NEW ENGLAND LEGENDS
AND FOLKLORE

Old Granary Burying Ground, Boston, where sleep priests and patriots, whose deeds became legends

New England Legends and Folklore

Based on Writings by
Samuel Adams Drake and Others,
and Illustrated with Photographs
by SAMUEL CHAMBERLAIN

Edited, with a Foreword,
by Harry Hansen

HASTINGS HOUSE   *Publishers*   NEW YORK

First published November, 1967
Second printing October, 1968

Adapted, with additions, from *A Book of New England Legends and Folk Lore,* by Samuel Adams Drake, published by Roberts Brothers, 1884.

Cape Cod Towns is adapted from a paper contributed by Katharine Lee Bates to *Historic Towns of New England,* edited by Lyman P. Powell, published by G. P. Putnam's Sons, 1898.

CONTENTS

6 CONTENTS

LEGEND AND REALITY:
A FOREWORD

A CENTURY has passed since Samuel Adams Drake wandered
through the towns of the New England seaboard and over
the old post roads, collecting and transcribing folk tales. Some of
the legends he found were based on actual occurrences in the remote colonial past: others were derived from the behavior of per-
sonalities who had made lasting impressions as governors, divines,
military captains, mariners and even lawbreakers. As the accounts
were communicated orally, there was much embellishment by
storytellers that was rejected later by more formal historians. Poets
of the era, turning legendary material into narrative verse, did not
feel bound by the fruits of what a later generation was to call research. The New England poets — Longfellow, Whittier, Oliver
Wendell Holmes, J. G. Brainard and James T. Fields, exercised
their own metrical license, yet somewhere in the text the core of
fact survived.

Drake complained that the "household poets" of his day used
legendary lore so effectively that the public frequently knew no
other version. It was this expansion of legend that made necessary

corrections of Longfellow's account of Paul Revere's Ride and
Whittier's spurious exchange of Civil War courtesies between
Stonewall Jackson and Barbara Frietche. Whittier himself ac-
knowledged that he had little on which to base that episode. Simi-
larly he accepted a popular mistaken version of the behavior of
Skipper Ireson, recounted in the chapter, *Marblehead One Hundred
Years Ago*, turning out what Drake describes as "the most idiosyn-
cratic ballad of purely home origin in the language." For this
Whittier also made amends to his friend Samuel Roads, author of
History and Traditions of Marblehead, saying he had used the
legend without knowing the actual circumstances.

Drake made allowance for the use of legends, but qualified
it by saying the poems "were not so much designed to teach history
or its truth, as to illustrate the spirit in an effective and picturesque
manner." This prompted him to write his own prose accounts, "in
order that those interested, more especially teachers, might have as
ready access to the truth as hitherto they have had to the romance
of history."

Whatever the reason, the human imagination had free play
in New England. For the most part it was concerned with things
violent, tragic and grim. However pleasing the landscape, life was
often hard, and the overbearing masters, whether political or theo-
cratic, made it harder. There was more hellfire and damnation than
compassion in the preaching. In the dark recesses of Puritan the-
ology the devil was strongly personified. Insecure persons watched
for the cloven hoof and declared they had smelled brimstone. It
was easy to attribute the devil's malevolence to women who irri-
tated the domineering males and the envious womenfolk.

The stain of persecution for witchcraft rests indelibly on New
England and especially on Salem, where the principal trials were
held and twenty innocent men and women were executed in 1692.
The compression of historic events into small compass accounts
for this emphasis on Salem, when many other communities were
also afflicted by the "great delusion." An investigation of charges

of witchcraft took place at Springfield, "on the Connecticut River," about 1645, and subsequently there were inquiries and some executions in Charlestown, Boston, Dorchester and Cambridge. In 1662 a woman was executed at Hartford, which, Thomas Hutchinson reminds the reader in his *History of the Province of Massachusetts Bay,* "was about thirty miles from Springfield, upon the same river." He writes that "more than an hundred women, many of them of fair characters and of the most reputable families, in the towns of Salem, Beverly, Andover, Billerica, etc., were apprehended, examined and generally committed to prison."

The Boston and Salem episodes compounded the offense by the stark contrast to the spirit of freedom in worship with which posterity associates the Puritan settlements. It must be taken into account, however, that this freedom did not mean defiance of religious authority, as Anne Hutchinson found out when she challenged the theocracy. Moreover, belief in witchcraft and the devil's malign influence did not begin in New England, nor end with the hangings. In Europe this superstition was originally associated with the uprooting of heresy, which poisoned human relations for centuries. In England and Scotland witch hunting flourished in the seventeenth century. Vernon Louis Parrington blamed the years of "stark reaction" on the long period of repression, which tried "to imprison the natural man in a straitjacket of Puritan righteousness." But repression brought revolt; it was the New England of the intolerant Cotton Mather that also produced the most intractable individualist in Roger Williams.

In a community habituated to clerical warnings against the machinations of the devil, reason was further unsettled when many of the accused confessed themselves guilty. Hutchinson writes: "Instead of suspecting and sifting the witnesses and suffering them to be cross-examined, the authority were imprudent in making use of leading questions and thereby putting words into their mouths and suffering others to do it . . . No wonder the whole country was in a consternation, when persons of sober lives and unblemished characters were committed to prison upon such sort of evidence. The most effectual way to prevent an accusation was to become an accuser, and accordingly the number of the afflicted increased every day and the number of the accused in proportion, who in general persisted in their innocency, but being strongly urged to give glory to God by their confession, and intimation being given that this was the only way to save their lives, and their friends urging them to do it, some were brought to own their guilt."

What amazed Hutchinson in the 18th century has become common political practice in the 20th. The informer who tells on his neighbors and even on his own family, and the innocent man who accuses himself, play important parts in the repressive measures of totalitarian states.

In tracing the basis for the witchcraft craze, the influence of books is rarely mentioned. It is known, however, that records and histories of witchcraft trials in England had reached New England. Governor Hutchinson says that the "bewitched" children of Parson Parris' household behaved exactly as others in England had done, when they fell into fits upon seeing the women they had accused. Nor were trance-like seizures associated solely with evil. Spiritual communication was often accompanied by manifestations of physical contortions. Young girls with seizures were part of the Shaker movement in New York State in the 1830's, and the influence they professed was not malevolent.

No doubt Hawthorne's genius has contributed to the sharpness of the Puritan persecutions in the public memory, especially since his writings were so widely disseminated in the public schools. Hawthorne considered the Salem witch trials part of a "universal madness," and Edward Wagenknecht, in his study, *Nathaniel Hawthorne, Man and Writer*, concludes that perhaps the author was so severe in his condemnation because he had to purge himself in his own mind of the sins of his ancestors. Wagenknecht says further that Hawthorne "is equally clear in his condemnation of Quaker persecutions as such, but in his most elaborate treatment of this theme, *The Gentle Boy*, he condemns Quaker fanaticism quite as strongly as Puritan intolerance." Whether or not Hawthorne was justified in this extreme judgment, there is plenty of evidence that the Quakers of the seventeenth century did not always turn the other cheek when they were abused. An example is the conduct of Mary Dyer (or Dier) who baited the authorities endlessly. True, they had besmirched her character violently for standing beside Anne Hutchinson in her trial; they had accused Mary of giving birth to a monster in order to blacken her as a member of the community. Mary did not choose to abide in the Rhode Island wilderness, but returned to Boston to speak her mind, and to suffer the extreme penalty.

The Puritans, who had fought for several generations to attain the freedom of worship they now possessed in New England, permitted no deviations from their own stern rule. The administration of the Massachusetts Bay Colony was especially incensed against members of the Society of Friends, and enforced its rulings by applying whips, lopping off ears, and imposing the humiliation of the pillory. Quakers who proved most intractable were banished from the Colony; four who returned were promptly hanged, as the law had provided. Therefore no legend of those years was more cherished by surviving Quakers than the account of how several of their number obtained a royal order taking the prosecution of Quakers out of the hands of the Colonial governor. Whether Charles II issued the order from hatred of the Puritans, or from a desire to see justice done, does not dim the fine dramatic character of the narrative.

Superstitions of a milder sort, that do not end in tragedy, grow out of man's attempt to cope with forces he cannot understand. Few lives are planned, and accident plays a large part in the vagaries of fortune. In modern life attempts have been made to subject premonitions and forebodings to rigorous tests and thus to apply the criteria of science, but opinion is still divided between those who accept the evidence as conclusive and those who remain skeptical. Drake recognized that rural communities which had grown from the Puritan migrations were burdened with a heavy baggage of superstitions, some of which had been brought from the mother country. Looking about him in the early 1880's, he was smugly satisfied that Americans were living in a practical age, "owing no allegiance whatsoever to that degrading thralldom of ancient superstition, but coldly rejecting everything that cannot be fully accounted for on rational grounds." He would, however, off-set this easygoing assumption by citing a few reminders of oddities of conduct that still persisted. His examples show what changes have taken place since his time. He wrote: "You will seldom see a man so much in a hurry that he will not stop to pick up a horse-shoe. One sees this ancient charm against evil spirits in every household." But the discarded horseshoe practically has disap-peared from our roads, and as a symbol survives only on goodluck cards. "Very few maidens neglect the opportunity to get a peep at the new moon over the right shoulder," writes Drake; but urban life has no time for it.

More longlived are the evil connotations of thirteen. "I know people who could not be induced to sit with thirteen at the table," he continues; "who consider spilling the salt as unlucky, and who put faith in dreams." In the middle of the twentieth century build-ers of office structures and hotels still omit designating a floor thirteen in the most worldly of cities, but no such handicap is at-tached in the public mind to streets and houses using that number, and many buildings name a thirteenth floor without incurring loss of rental income. Dreams, however, are more significant today than in former times, but it is the dreambook of Sigmund Freud, and not Napoleon's, that we consult. We must admit Drake has a point when he says "the familiar legend of the hedgehog (ground-hog) remains a trusted indication of an early or late spring," al-though it is more a subject of amusement than belief. This belongs with folklore of the weather, a subject closely allied with soothsaying, and evoking the incriminations visited on that unsatisfactory practice.

Joseph H. Choate, the great jurist, was born in Salem in 1832 and cherished memories of customs he had known in boyhood. In an autobiographical sketch he wrote:

"Like the other towns on the eastern shore of Massachusetts, which were all of purely English origin, Salem must have retained by tradition many usages of transatlantic origin or derived from the customs of the first settlers. For instance, the curfew bell, which, I believe, still rings regularly as it has for the last 275 years, was certainly an importation from the old country, and the town crier must have been of similar origin. He was employed to give notices of sales, losses of children, losses of dogs, and other important local events. He carried a handbell and would stop at each corner as he passed down Essex Street and ring the bell with all his might, and we gathered about him with great interest to hear the news, as with a stentorian voice that could be heard the length of a block he would utter his important intelligence. And then there was the local vendor, a quaint old Frenchman, Old Monarque, who dealt in a very limited number of articles as he drove his pushcart all about the town, shouting in broken English: 'Pickeldy limes and tamadirinds, two for a cent apiece.' This, too, must have been an old English mode of advertising before the days of newspapers."

One of the legends in this collection, that of the stone-throwing devil of Portsmouth is practically the prototype of oft-repeated folk tales of this kind. The reader will recognize in it his familiar friend, the *Poltergeist*, the inexplicable mischief-maker who starts knocking on doors, rapping on walls, and overturning furniture in unexpected places. Within recent years such unaccountable antics were reported by a family in a Long Island village and provided New York newspapers with an opportunity to beguile readers with new versions of supernatural visitations.

The seacoast towns of New England had long memories of

disasters. Here the winter storms lashed the sailing vessels coming in with a catch from the fishing areas. The rockbound coast was no picturesque embellishment; it was a real hazard. Big and little vessels foundered on the sharp outcroppings of rock and were pounded to pieces within sight of land. The fate of skippers was a household legend and the presence of widows a cruel reminder. The poets found themes in these tragedies and in Drake's day Longfellow made the reef of Norman's Woe and the wreck of the *Hesperus* familiar to schoolboys across the country. Whittier also used as a subject a disaster off the Isle of Shoals. Sometimes the legends recounted a captain's courage, but more often they recorded the devil's handiwork.

The hardships imposed on mariners and fishermen by the sea are reflected in Katharine Lee Bates' descriptions of the Cape Cod settlements at the turn of the century. Men who had grown old whale-hunting were still sitting before their cottages recalling the hazards of their vanished occupation, and Provincetown was still a haven for Portuguese fisherfolk instead of poets and playwrights. The old families and the younger immigrants made a precarious living from the sea, but today the peninsula of Cape Cod is the recreation ground of thousands who gain their livelihood elsewhere and find pure enjoyment sitting in front of their white-painted cottages in the sunshiny land of the dunes.

HARRY HANSEN

LEGENDS OF SALEM

IN NEW ENGLAND no town except Plymouth takes precedence of Salem in the order of settlement, a fact of which her citizens are naturally as proud as an old family is of ancestry going back to the Conquest. The political and commercial fortunes of Salem have been singularly alike. Roger Conant, the founder, leader of a forlorn hope, was eclipsed by John Endicott, who in turn was overshadowed by John Winthrop — a man quick to see that no place was large enough to contain three governors, two of them deposed, one in authority, and all ambitious to lead the Puritan vanguard in the great crusade of the century. The site was not approved. He therefore sought out a new one at Boston, to which the seat of government was presently removed. The halls of the Essex Institute contain many interesting relics of the time when Salem played an important part in Colonial history.

In respect to the commercial importance of Salem, which at one time was very great — ships in the Hoogly and the Yangtse, ships at Ceylon and Madagascar, ships on the Gold Coast, in Polynesia and Vancouver — you can hardly put a thought on the wide seas where there were not ships flying, an importance so great that its merchants were called King this and King that, while by reason of the frequent intercourse had with those "far countrees," its society took a tone and color almost Oriental. Yet, when its great rival overshadowed it, Salem was converted from a seaport of the first rank into a modestly flourishing place of manufactures. In the cabinets of the Peabody Museum the visitor sees a thousand evidences of its ancient commercial renown.

The two most noteworthy things that have happened in Salem are the witchcraft persecution and the birth of Nathaniel Hawthorne. Without suspecting it, the traveler who arrives by the usual route is at once ushered upon the scene of a tragedy in which the guilty escaped and the innocent were punished. Just out of the city, on its southern skirt, the railway passes within view of an uncouth heap of steep-sided gray rocks, moderately high, on whose windy summit a few houses make a group of dusky silhouettes. This is a sort of waste place, good neither for planting, grazing, or building. Long ago, so long that no living man remembers it, one solitary tree grew upon that wind-swept height. But at length it sickened and died; and after contending a while with the wintry blasts, the withered skeleton of a tree was cut down and burned. Those cold gray ledges where it stood is Gallows Hill. The tree, tradition says, was that upon which the condemned witches were hung. This was the setting in 1884.

Upon entering the city, the great high-road running north and south takes the more ambitious name of street. Upon reaching the heart of the city, it expands into a public square, or the old town market-place. As he advances towards the center the curious visitor may still see the quaint old house in which Roger Williams lived, and in which tradition says that some of the witchcraft examinations were held; in the Square he has arrived in the region, half real, half romantic, described in Hawthorne's tales *Main Street, A Rill from the Town-Pump,* and *Endicott and the Red Cross,* of which latter this is a fragment:

A pioneer dwelling in Salem, reproduced with stocks and pillory

"The central object in the mirrored picture was an edifice of humble architecture, with neither steeple nor bell to proclaim it — what nevertheless it was — the house of prayer. A token of the perils of the wilderness was seen in the grim head of a wolf which had just been slain within the precincts of the town, and, according to the regular mode of claiming the bounty, was nailed to the porch of the meeting-house. The blood was still plashing on the door-step.

"In close vicinity to the sacred edifice appeared that important engine of Puritanic authority, the whipping-post — with the soil around it well trodden by the feet of evil-doers, who had there been disciplined. At one corner of the meeting-house was the pillory, and at the other the stocks; and, by a singular good fortune, for our sketch, the head of an Episcopalian and suspected Catholic was grotesquely incased in the former machine; while a fellow-criminal who had boisterously quaffed a health to the King was confined by the legs in the latter."

But this picture is only the grimly humorous prelude to another of a very different nature, upon which is founded that story of sin, remorse, and shame, *The Scarlet Letter.*

In the throng surrounding the culprits, "there was likewise a young woman with no mean share of beauty, whose doom it was to wear the letter 'A' on the breast of her gown, in the eyes of all the world and her own children. And even her own children knew what that initial signified. Sporting with her infamy, the lost and desperate creature had embroidered the fatal token in scarlet cloth with golden thread and the nicest art of needlework, so that the capital A might have been thought to mean Admirable, or anything rather than Adulteress."

Hawthorne tells us that he found the missive from which this incident is drawn in the room occupied by him in the Salem Custom House while he was serving as surveyor of the port under the veteran General James Miller, the hero of Lundy's Lane. In one respect, therefore, the novelist's life has its analogy to that of Charles Lamb, following whom in his inimitable monologue on the South Sea House, which forms the initial chapter to the *Essays of Elia* our own countryman, though in a different spirit,

Birthplace of Nathaniel Hawthorne, Salem. "A humble dwelling, with humble surroundings," swept by winds from the sea

The Old Custom House in Salem where, in the lazy hours between cargoes, the Young Surveyor of the Port found inspiration for *The Scarlet Letter*

The House of the Seven Gables. The seven gables, said Hawthorne, were "a whole sisterhood of edifices, breathing through the spiracles of one great chimney."

sketches the Old Custom House and its corps of superannuated weighers, gaugers, and tide-waiters as the introductory chapter to *The Scarlet Letter.*

This old red-brick edifice, if we except a later renovation of its interior, stands precisely as it did in the novelist's time, — the prominent object in a region which has seen better days. The same flag waves from the staff, the same eagle extends its gilded wings above the roof. The novelist describes it in a grimly satirical way as an asylum for decayed politicians, who dozed and slept in easy tranquility during the hours nominally devoted to business, there being little to do, except to keep up the appearance of official regularity. The surveyor cuts his portraits with a diamond. His desk, showing the marks of a nervous or an idle hand visible in many lines and gashes upon it, is preserved among the curiosities of Plummer Hall.

Not far from the Custom House, in a narrow by-street, is the ancient wooden tenement in which the novelist was born. We pass, as it were, through a corner of the eighteenth century, of which this house is indubitably a relic. It is an humble dwelling, with humble surroundings. Here he wrote many of the shorter tales, that it is entirely safe to say have now more readers than when they first saw the light, and many more tales he says were committed to the flames; here he kept that long and weary vigil while waiting for the slow dawning of his fame; and here he tells us that it was won.

To these early struggles, ending with repeated disappointment, is doubtless to be ascribed the indifference with which Hawthorne speaks of the city of his birth. He refers his return to it from time to time to a sort of fatality which he passively obeyed. Though he admits a certain languid attraction to it, we can hardly distinguish it from repulsion, so intimately do these opposite feelings mingle in the current. Yet the same hand that penned *The House of the Seven Gables* and *The Old Custom House,* puts the

The so-called Witch House of Salem, once lived in by Judge Corwin, who presided at witchcraft trials.

early history of Salem in a nutshell in *Main Street;* and it also gave us those fascinating chapters of revery, *Sights from a Steeple* and *A Rill from the Town-Pump,* — all drawn from the associations of the master's birthplace.

The scarlet letter was one of those ingenious methods of punishment, almost satanic in their conception, which disgrace the criminal annals of the Colony. For different offences a different letter was prescribed, to be worn in private as in public — the wearer thus being made the living record of his or her own infamy. The drunkard wore a capital letter D, the criminal convicted of incest an I, of heresy an H, and of adultery an A, sewed on the arm or breast; and this accusing insignia was forbidden to be removed upon pain of a severer penalty. Many a poor sinner thus wore his heart upon his sleeve, "for daws to peck at."

The novelist, by instinct, seized upon one of the most striking episodes of the hard Puritan life. The scene of his tale is laid, not in Salem, but in Boston.

Although Hawthorne makes but slight use of witchcraft history in constructing *The House of the Seven Gables,* the opening chapter shows him to have been familiar with it. But notwithstanding the apparent adherence to truth, contrived with such consummate art as to fix the impression that the legend of the old Pyncheon family is derived from some authentic source, it will be better to regard the author's statement "that the reader, according to his own pleasure, may either disregard, or allow it to float imperceptibly about the characters and events for the sake of picturesque effect." Thus by freely availing himself of the names of actual personages whose history is artfully interwoven with actual occurrences, and again by associating these with local descriptions of rare fidelity, the effect of solid reality is produced, and the story proceeds on a chain of circumstantial evidence from the materials of his own rich fancy.

After this explanation it will be scarcely necessary to observe that the words which are put into the mouth of Matthew Maule at the moment he is ascending the fatal ladder, a condemned and abhorred wizard, and which form the underlying motive of *The House of the Seven Gables*, — the blight of an evil destiny passing from generation to generation, — were as a matter of fact really spoken by Sarah Good, not to Colonel Pyncheon, but to the Reverend Nicholas Noyes, who most cruelly embittered her last moments by telling her that she was a miserable witch. And it was to him she made the memorable reply that "if he took away her life, God would give him blood to drink."

There is, however, reason for supposing, since it has been so minutely described, that the House of the Seven Gables was at least suggested by that of Philip English, who was near becoming a martyr to the witchcraft horror himself. What is clearer still, is that the novelist has laid several of the old Colonial houses, both in Salem and Boston, under contribution for whatever might embellish his description, which is certainly no invention, but is a true picture of the early architecture even in its minutest details. But in such an unreal atmosphere as surrounds it, we are not sure that the house itself may not turn out to be an illusion of the mirage created by an effort of the weird romancer's will. Its appearance is thus portrayed in the opening words of the romance:

"There it rose, a little withdrawn from the line of the street, but in pride, not modesty. Its whole visible exterior was ornamented with quaint figures, conceived in the grotesqueness of a Gothic fancy, and drawn or stamped in the glittering plaster, composed of lime, pebbles, and bits of glass, with which the woodwork of the walls was overspread. On every side the seven gables pointed sharply towards the sky, and presented the aspect of a whole sisterhood of edifices, breathing through the spiracles of one great chimney. The many lattices, with their small, diamond-shaped panes, admitted the sunlight into hall and chamber, while nevertheless the second story, projecting far over the base, and itself retiring beneath the third, threw a shadowy and thoughtful gloom into the lower rooms. Carved globes of wood were affixed under the jutting stories. Little spiral rods of iron beautified each of the seven peaks. On the triangular portion of the gable, that fronted next the street, was a dial, put up that very morning, and on which the sun was still marking the passage of the first bright hour in a history that was not destined to be all so bright."

The house in Danvers in which lived Rebecca Nurse, victim of the witchcraft persecutions.

THE SALEM WITCHCRAFT TRAGEDY

*The flames of superstition that scorched the fair name of
Salem (Hebr. Sholem, Peace) did not flare up in the midst
of the city where later Hawthorne dreamed and McIntyre
planned. They were ignited in Salem Village, a settlement in
the environs, whither the founder Roger Conant once led his
neighbors to evade the overbearing rule of Governor Winthrop. In the village church (there's a marker in Centre
Street) Cotton Mather denounced witches, and there the im-
mature daughter and niece of Parson Samuel Parris acted out
the seizures that damned the innocent. And here still stands
the house from which Rebecca Nurse was led to her doom on
Gallows Hill. In time this became* DANVERS, *a friendly community with more than concrete highways tying it to the city
of Salem. But eighty years ago Samuel Adams Drake saw it
as he describes it in the following sketch.*

THE PLACE where a great crime has been committed always has
something strangely fascinating about it. Accursed though it
may be, repulsive as its associations generally are, most people will

go a greater distance to see the locality of a murder than for any other purpose whatsoever. The house where a great man was born is often quite unknown and unvisited even in its own neighborhood; the house associated with a murder or a homicide is sharply remembered.

"We may lament, then," said Judge Joseph Story in his Centennial Address at Salem, "the errors of the times which led to these prosecutions [for witchcraft]. But surely our ancestors had no special reasons for shame in a belief which had the universal sanction of their own and all former ages; which counted in its train philosophers as well as enthusiasts; which was graced by the learning of prelates as well as the countenance of kings; which the law supported by its mandates, and the purest judges felt no compunctions in enforcing. Let Witch Hill remain forever memorable by this sad catastrophe, not to perpetuate our dishonor, but as an affecting, enduring proof of human infirmity, — a proof that perfect justice belongs to one judgment-seat only, — that which is linked to the throne of God."

What was this belief that had such high moral and legal sanction? It was this: that the Devil might and did personally appear to, enter into, and actively direct, the everyday life of men. And he did this without the intervention of any of those magical arts or conjurations once thought indispensable to induce him to appear. For this there was Scripture authority, chapter and verse. He was supposed to come sometimes in one form, sometimes in another, to tempt his victims with the promise that upon signing a contract to become his, both body and soul, they should want for nothing, and that he would undertake to revenge them upon all their enemies. The traditional witch was usually some decrepit old village crone, of a sour and malignant temper, as thoroughly hated as feared; but this did not exclude men from sharing in the power of becoming noted wizards, — though from the great number of women who were accused, it would appear that the arch-enemy usually preferred to try his arts upon the weaker and more impressible sex. The fatal compact was consummated by the victim registering his or her name in a book or upon a scroll of parchment, and with his own blood. The form of these contracts is nowhere preserved.

The bargain being concluded, Satan delivered to the new recruit an imp or familiar spirit, which sometimes had the form of a cat, at others of a mole, a bird, a miller-fly, or other insect or animal. Feeding, suckling or rewarding these imps was by the law of England declared a felony.

Witches, according to the popular belief, had the power to ride at will through the air on a broomstick or a spit, to attend distant meetings or sabbaths of witches; but for this purpose they must first have anointed themselves with a certain magical ointment given to them by the fiend.

In the course of those remarkable trials at Salem, several of the accused persons, in order to save their lives, confessed to having signed their names in the Devil's book, to having been baptized by him, and to having attended midnight meetings of witches, or sacraments held on the green near the minister's house, to which they came riding through the air. They admitted that he had sometimes appeared to them in the form of a black dog or cat, sometimes as a horse, once as a "fine grave man," but generally as a black man of severe aspect. It was generally held impossible for a witch to say the Lord's Prayer correctly, and it is a matter of record that one woman, while under examination, was put to this test, when it was noted that in one place she substituted some words of her own for those of the prayer. Such a failure of memory was considered, even by some learned judges, as a decisive proof of guilt. Even the trial of throwing a witch into the water, to see whether she would sink or swim, was once made in Connecticut.

The scene of the witchcraft outbreak of 1692 is an elevated knoll of no great extent, rising among the shaggy hills and spongy meadows that lie at some distance back from the more thickly settled part of the town of Danvers, Massachusetts, formerly Salem

Village. It is indeed a quiet little neighborhood to have made so much noise in the world. The first appearance of everything is so peaceful, so divested of all hurry or excitement, as to suggest an hereditary calm, — a pastoral continued from generation to generation. Then, as the purpose which has brought him hither comes into his mind, the visitor looks about him in doubt whether this can really be the locality of that fearful tragedy.

Here are the identical houses that were standing when those unheard-of events took place, still solemnly commemorating them, as if doomed to stand eternally. This village street is the same old highway through which the dreadful infection spread from house to house unto the remote corners of the ancient shire, until, as we read, there were forty men of Andover that could raise the devil as well as any astrologer. Here too is the site of the old meeting-house, in which those amazing scenes, the witchcraft examinations, took place. A little farther on we come to the spot of ground where the Parsonage with the lean-to chamber stood. The sunken outlines of the cellar were still to be seen, and even some relics of the house itself remained in the outbuildings attached to the Wadsworth mansion, which overlooks the Witch-Ground, and which was built in the same year that the old Parsonage was pulled down. It was in this Ministry House, as it was then called, that the circle of young girls met, whose denunciations, equivalent to the death-warrant of the accused person, soon overspread the land with desolation and woe; and it was here that the alleged midnight convocations of witches met to celebrate their unholy sacraments, and to renew their solemn league and covenant with Satan, in draughts of blood, and by inscribing their names in his fatal book.

It makes one sick at heart to think of a child only eleven years old, such as Abigail Williams was, taking away the lives of men and women who had always borne unblemished reputations among their friends and neighbors, by identifying them as having attended these meetings, and of having hurt this or that person. These poor creatures could scarcely understand that they were seriously accused by one so young of a crime made capital by the law. But their doubts were soon removed. Once they were accused, every man's hand was against them. Children testified against their own parents, husbands against their wives, wives against their husbands, neighbors against neighbor. One's blood alternately boils and freezes while reading the damning evidence of the record to the fatal infatuation of the judges, to their travesty of justice, to their pitiless persecution of the prisoners at the bar, and to the overmastering terror that silenced the voice of humanity in this stricken community. Panic reigned everywhere supreme. It is an amazing history, but, incredible as it seems, it is all true.

The main features of these trials are so familiar that it will only be necessary to repeat that hundreds of innocent persons were thrown into prison, while twenty were barbarously executed, at the instance of some girls of the Village, who went into violent convulsions, real or pretended, as soon as they were confronted with the prisoners at the bar. The convictions were had upon spectral evidence, which meant weight was to be given to the effect. The strange antics of the possessed girls were considered proof of the criminal power of witchcraft in the accused in the absence of a visible cause. The statute assumed that this power could only proceed from a familiarity or compact with the Evil One, and punished it with death. The evidence, however, was of two kinds. When interrogated by the magistrates, the girls first gave their evidence calmly, like ordinary witnesses to the criminal acts, and then went into their spasms, which all believed were caused by the prisoners. Their incoherent ravings and outcries were also accepted as good and valid testimony. It must be added that Cotton Mather, despite his eagerness to stamp out witchcraft, distrusted spectral evidence and warned against its introduction. When, however, the court admitted it, he acquiesced.

Though humanity may well revolt at the explanation, the theory that imposture was maintained by these girls of Salem Village, is the one we turn from in dismay as a thing not proved, or even admitted, but as a haunting probability that will not down at our bidding. Governor Thomas Hutchinson was unable to give a positive judgment. In his *History of the Province of Massachusetts Bay* he tells what became of the two girls, aged 9 and 11, who caused so much tragedy in Salem. He says: "The children returned to their ordinary behavior, lived to adult age, made profession of religion, and the affliction they had been under they publicly declared to be one motive for it. One of them I knew many years after. She had the character of a very sober, virtuous woman, and never made any acknowledgment of fraud in this transaction."

Assembly House, Salem

THE ESCAPE OF PHILIP ENGLISH

Philip English proved to be Salem's most enterprising and successful citizen. He built and owned twenty-seven vessels and carried on a great commercial trade, acquired large tracts of land, some of them through his wife, and built at the foot of Essex Street, overlooking the harbor across to the Beverly shore and the Marblehead shore, a fine old gabled house of large dimensions for that day, besides fourteen other valuable houses. . . . When the witchcraft delusion broke out in 1692 his eminence and great success brought upon him and his wife, probably because of envy at their success and high character, the charge of being guilty of witchcraft. They were both arrested and lodged in Boston jail, from which they managed to escape and took refuge in New York City. But so rapidly did the delusion die out when the awful bubble had once burst, that on their return in the following year they are said to have been welcomed home with bonfires and other marks of rejoicing. Certainly my ancestor was extremely fortunate to escape with his life. I read that, not finding his per-

son, they seized upon and confiscated £1,500 worth of his
goods, and after many years he recovered judgment against
the marshal for £60 and was awarded £200 by the Common-
wealth for his indemnity, a very sorry satisfaction for all his
suffering.

JOSEPH H. CHOATE

DURING THE time of the witchcraft delusion at Salem Village, the victims in nearly every case were people in the humblest walk of life. Philip English of Salem was the first person of superior station to be attainted by this persecution, which, like a wolf that is maddened by the taste of blood, began to grow bolder in pursuit of its victims.

Philip English had emigrated to America from the island of Jersey. Having found a home in the family of William Hollingsworth, a wealthy inhabitant of Salem, he formed the acquaintance of Hollingsworth's only child, Susanna, who, besides having received an education superior to the usual requirements of that day, possessed rare endowments of mind and person. The acquaintance ripened into mutual affection and in due time Philip English married the daughter of his friend and patron. He, too, became in time a rich and eminent merchant.

In April, 1692, the terrible accusation fell like a thunderbolt upon this happy home. The wife and mother was the first victim to the credulity or malignity of her neighbors. In the night the officer entered her bedchamber, read his fatal warrant and then surrounded the house with guards, intending to carry her to prison in the morning. Mrs. English gave herself up for lost. With supreme heroism, however, she gathered her stricken family together in the morning to its usual devotions, gave directions for the education of her children, clasped them to her bosom, and commending them and herself to God, bade them farewell. She was then taken by the sheriff before the sitting magistrates, Hathorne and

Curwen, who committed her to Salem jail as a witch. Her firmness is memorable. A little later her husband was also accused by a poor bedridden creature. He concealed himself for a time; but at length he came forward, gave himself up, and demanded the privilege of sharing his wife's fate. The two were immured in the same dungeon to await the solemn farce of a trial. The prison being crowded to overflowing, English and his wife were, through the intercession of friends, removed to the jail in Boston, where for six weeks they endured the dismal prospect of dying together upon the scaffold.

But fortunately for them, and in consequence, doubtless, of the fact that English was a merchant of property, and a person of known probity, he and his unfortunate wife were admitted to bail, being allowed the privilege of the town by day, on condition of punctually returning to the prison at night, to be locked up again until the following morning. Though rendering their condition more tolerable, this did not make it the less hopeless. They were

The Ropes Mansion in Salem

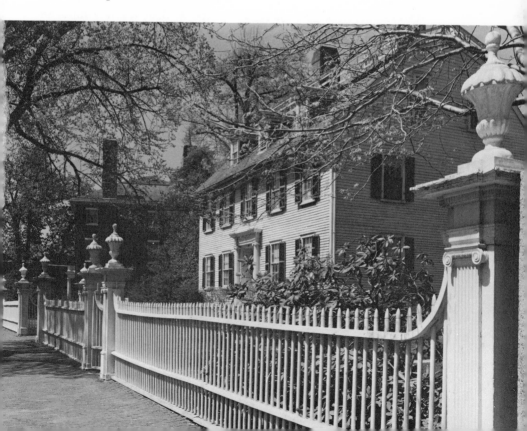

visited in their prison by some of the most eminent clergymen of
the town, one of whom, the Reverend Joshua Moody, manifested
the deepest interest in their spiritual and temporal welfare. This
good man, whose sound head refused to admit the prevailing delusion, while his equally sound heart fitted him for deeds of mercy,
went to the prison on the day before English and his wife were to
be taken back to Salem for trial, and invited them to attend public
worship in his church. They went.

When he ascended the pulpit, the clergyman announced as
his text this verse, having a peculiar significance to two of his
hearers: "If they persecute you in one city, flee into another!"

In his discourse, the preacher justified every attempt to escape
from the forms of justice when justice itself was being violated in
them. After the service was over, the minister again visited the
prisoners in their cell, and asked English pointedly whether he had
detected the meaning of his sermon of the morning. English hesi-
tating to commit himself, Moody frankly told him that his own
life and that of his wife were in danger, and that he, looking this in
the face, ought to provide for an escape without losing a moment.
English could not believe it; it was too monstrous. "God will not
suffer them to hurt me," he said in this conviction.

"What," exclaimed his wife, "do you not think that they who
have suffered already were innocent?"

"Yes."

"Why, then, may we not suffer also? Take Mr. Moody's ad-
vice; let us fly."

To make an end of this indecision, proceeding from the fear
that flight would be quickly construed to mean guilt, Moody then
unfolded his plan. He told the reluctant English that everything
necessary for his escape had been already provided: that the Governor, Sir William Phips, was in the secret, and countenanced it;
that the jailer had his instructions to open the prison doors; and
that, finally, all being in readiness, at midnight a conveyance, furnished by friends who were in the plot, would come to carry them

From Salem's prosperous days; The Peirce-Nichols House

away to a place of security. In fact every precaution that prudence could suggest or foresee, or that influence in high places could secure, had been taken in order to prevent the shedding of innocent blood. He procured letters, under Sir William's own hand and seal, to Governor Fletcher of New York, thus providing for the fugitives, first a safeguard, and next an inviolable asylum. Finally, he told English plainly that if he did not carry his wife off, he, Moody, would do so himself. The affair was arranged on the spot.

At the appointed time the prison doors were unbarred, the prisoners came out, and while the solemn stillness of midnight brooded over the afflicted town, they fled from persecution in one city to another.

Governor Fletcher took the homeless wanderers into his own mansion, where he made them welcome, not as fugitives from justice, but as exiles fleeing from persecution. They were entertained as the most honored of guests. The next year Philip English returned home. The storm of madness had passed by, leaving its terrible marks in many households. His own was destined to feel its consequences in a way to turn all his joy into sorrow. Within two years from the time Mrs. English was torn from her home to answer the charge of felony, she died of the cruel treatment she had received. Moody's course was commended by all discerning men, but he felt the angry resentment of the multitude, among whom were some persons of high rank. In consequence he returned to his old charge at Portsmouth, New Hampshire, the next year after his successful interposition to save Mr. and Mrs. English from the executioner's hands.

Such is the tradition long preserved in the English family. Philip English's granddaughter became Susanna Hathorne — which was the original way of spelling the name subsequently borne by the novelist. Nathaniel Hawthorne had thus on one side for an ancestor the implacable persecutor of those to whom he was afterward to be related by intermarriage, thus furnishing the idea he has so ingeniously worked out in *The House of the Seven Gables*.

ROBERT CALEF, THE MAN WHO DEFIED WITCHCRAFT AND COTTON MATHER

THE ACTIVE agency of Satan in human affairs being admitted, it became the bounden duty of the godly ministers to meet his insidious attacks upon the churches, and they, as men deeply learned in such things, were naturally appealed to by magistrates and judges for help and guidance. It was declared from the pulpit that the devil was making a most determined effort to root out the Christian religion in New England, and the government was advised vigorously to prosecute the cases of witchcraft before it.

Cotton Mather was the foremost clergyman of that dark day. He directed all his great abilities and learning energetically to exterminate the devils who, as he tells in his *Wonders of the Invisible World,* were walking about the streets "with lengthened chains, making a dreadful noise, while brimstone was making a horrid and hellish stench" in men's nostrils. Learned, eloquent, and persuasive, a man of great personal magnetism and large following, his influence was sure to be potential on whichever side it might be cast. It was now thrown with all its force, not to avert but to strengthen the delusion, thereby aggravating its calamitous consequences.

Against Mather, neighbor, adviser, and bosom friend of Governor Sir William Phips, and acknowledged head of the New England clergy in its highest spiritual estate, now appeared Robert Calef, a clothier unknown outside of his own obscure neighborhood. Calef addressed letters to Mather, in which he arraigned not only the witchcraft proceedings, but the delusion itself, the occasion being one Margaret Rule, a young woman of Mather's own congregation, whose singular afflictions had just been published to the world by him under the startling caption of *Another Brand Pluckt from the Burning.* According to Mather this young woman was haunted by no fewer than eight malignant spectres, led on by a principal demon, who upon her refusal to enter into a bond with him, continually put her in excruciating bodily torture by pinching, scorching and sticking pins into her flesh, throwing her into convulsions, lifting her bodily off the bed, and the like, wherein, says Mather, she languished "for just six weeks together." And we are also told that at times the spectators of her miseries would be nearly choked by the fumes of brimstone rising in her chamber.

Taking the alarm, which many no doubt equally shared, Calef seems to have distrusted either the integrity or the wisdom of his learned adversary, whom he now opposed in behalf of religion and public policy, not only with ability and vigor, but with a surprisingly well-equipped arsenal of scriptural learning. In vain Mather sneeringly spoke of him as "the weaver turned minister." Calef only plied him the more pointedly. At the end of the controversy the despised clothier turned out to be one of those men whose reason is never overthrown by panic, and who do not recede a single inch. Mather began with the mistake of underrating him as an antagonist.

After Mather's story of Margaret Rule had been made public, Calef also drew up and circulated one, taken from the mouths of other eye-witnesses, which was a protest against the methods used by Mather to draw out extravagant and incoherent statements from the afflicted girl. This proceeding gave great offence to the reverend author of the *Wonders*. He retorted with abusive epithets and threatened Calef with an action for slander. Calef was, in fact, arrested on a warrant for uttering "scandalous libels," and bound over for trial, but no prosecutor appearing, the case was dismissed.

Instead of being silenced, Calef pursued with unremitting pertinacity his purpose to prevent a new access of the dismal frenzy of the preceding year, which he terms, with strong feeling, "the sorest affliction and greatest blemish to religion that ever befell this country." Later on Mather condescended to reply, but it is evident that the reaction had now set in, and that those who had been the most forward in abetting the witchcraft proceedings were anxiously considering how best to exculpate themselves both to their own and to the newly awakened public conscience. Mather was no exception. Favored by this reaction, Calef continued to press him hard. Cotton Mather's story of Margaret Rule is, in fact, a plea and an apology for the past. In it he asks, "Why, after all my unwearied cares and pains to rescue the miserable from the lions and bears of hell, which had seized them, and after all my studies to disappoint the devils in their designs to confound my neighborhood, must I be driven to the necessity of an apology?" This language shows how hard it was for him to be forced to descend from his high pedestal.

But witchcraft had now indeed got to the length of its blood-corroded chain, and while the belief still prevailed almost as strongly as ever, few men could be found bold enough to advocate it openly. The sickening reflection that the judges had decreed the death of a score of innocent persons upon a mistake paralyzed men's tongues, unless, like Calef, they spoke in obedience to the command of conscience. In 1700 he collected and had printed in London all the pieces relating to his controversy with Cotton Mather, to which were added an *Impartial Account* of the Salem outbreak, and a review of Mather's life of Sir William Phips. To this he gave the title *More Wonders of the Invisible World*. No printer could be found in Boston or in the Colony to undertake the publication or expose it for sale. It was publicly burned in the College Yard at Cambridge by order of the president, whom its exposures reached through his near-relative. To break its force a vindication was prepared and printed, but there were no more denunciations for witchcraft, or courts assembled to hang innocent people. Robert Calef indeed felt the resentment of the Mathers, but he had saved the cause.

King's Chapel, Boston

MARY DYER,
A QUAKER AMONG PURITANS

IT IS A MATTER of history that in 1656 a people who wore their hair long, kept their hats on in the public assemblies, and who said *thee* and *thou* instead of *you* when addressing another person, made their unwelcome appearance in New England. They were forthwith attacked with all the energy of a bitter persecution.

When called upon to speak out in defense of their cruel proceedings, the Puritan authorities declared their creed to be this: They having established themselves in a wilderness in order to enjoy undisturbed their own religious convictions, held it right to exclude all others who might seek to introduce different opinions, and therefore discord, among them. From this it is plain to see that the ideal of toleration had not yet been born. The further fact that to this cruel and selfish policy, sternly preserved in to the last, the Colony owed the loss of most of the political privileges it had hitherto enjoyed, renders it one of the stepping-stones of history.

On both sides of the ocean the Puritan cry was "Freedom to worship God as we do." The persecution of Quakers had already begun in England under the austere rule of the Puritan Commonwealth. They were treated as weak fanatics who needed wholesome correction, rather than as persons dangerous to the public weal. After this had been some time in progress, some of the persecuted Friends came over to New England for an asylum, or out of the frying-pan into the fire. The local authorities, urged on by the whole body of orthodox ministers, resolved to strangle this new heresy in its cradle. But they had forgotten the story of the dragon's teeth. For every Quaker they banished, ten rose in his place.

The situation of the Quakers in New England is summarized in Morse and Parrish's *History of New England* thus:

"In 1656 began what has been generally called the persecution of the Quakers. The first who openly professed the principles of this sect in this colony were Mary Fisher and Ann Austin, who came from Barbados in July of this year. A few weeks after nine others arrived in the ship *Speedwell* of London. On the 8th of September they were brought before the Court of Assistants. It seems they had beforehand affirmed that they were sent by God to reprove the people for their sins; they were accordingly questioned how they could make it appear that God sent them? After pausing they answered that they had the same call that Abraham had to go out of his country. To other questions they gave rude and contemptuous answers, which is the reason assigned for committing them to prison. A great number of their books, which they brought over with intent to scatter them about the country, were seized and reserved for the fire. Soon after this, as the Governor was going from public worship on the Lord's Day to his own house, Mary Prince called to him from a window of the prison, railing at and reviling him, saying: 'Woe unto thee, thou art an oppressor' and denouncing the judgments of God upon him. The Governor sent for her twice from the prison to his house, and took much pains to persuade her to desist from such extravagancies. Two of the ministers were present, and with much moderation and tenderness endeavored to convince her of her errors, to which she returned with the grossest railings, reproaching them as hirelings, deceivers of the people, Baal's priests, the seed of the serpent, of the brood of Ishmael, and the like.

"At this time there was no special provision made in the laws for the punishment of the Quakers. But in virtue of a law against heretics in general, the court passed sentence of banishment upon them all. Afterwards other severe laws were enacted, among which were the following: any Quaker after the first conviction, if a man, was to lose one ear, and for the second offense, the other; a woman to be each time severely whipped, and the third time, whether man or woman, to have their tongues bored through with a redhot iron. In October, 1658, the members of the general court of Massachusetts, by a majority of one vote only, passed a law for punishing with death all Quakers who should return to their jurisdiction after banishment. Under this law four persons were executed."

Mary Dyer, a comely and grave matron, then living in Rhode Island, was one of those rare spirits who are predestined to become martyrs and saints to the faith that they profess.

She and her husband, William Dyer, were originally inhabitants of Boston, and members of the church there, they having emigrated from England to the Colony in 1635. It is clear that both she and her husband belonged to the better class of emigrants. She is represented by Sewel, the Quaker historian, as a person of good family and estate, and by John Winthrop as a very proper and fair woman, but, as he deprecatingly adds, having a "very proud spirit." In her, therefore, we have the portrait of a comely woman of fine presence, high spirit, a fair share of education, and possessing, moreover, a soul endowed with the purpose of an evangelist or, at need, a martyr. Both Mrs. Dyer and her husband became early converts to the peculiar doctrines held by that priestess of common sense, Mrs. Anne Hutchinson, to whose untoward fortunes they continued steadfast. There was, in fact, a bond of sympathy between these two women. When Mrs. Hutchinson was excommunicated, young Mrs. Dyer walked out of the church with her in presence of the whole congregation. When she was banished in 1637, Mrs. Dyer followed her to Rhode Island.

During the excitement produced by the rapid spread of Mrs. Hutchinson's opinions, and by her subsequent arrest and trial on the charge of heresy, Mrs. Dyer gave premature birth, it was said, to a monster, which Winthrop describes with nauseating minuteness. Losing sight of Mrs. Dyer for nearly twenty years, we next see the comely young wife as a middle-aged matron, blindly obeying the command of destiny. She now presents herself in the garb of a Quaker, and in company with professing Quakers, to the people of Boston, any one of whom, by harboring her even for a single night, or offering her a crust of bread, became a breaker of the law and liable to a heavy penalty. She was immediately taken up and thrust into the common jail, where she remained in confinement until her husband hastened to her relief. His prayer for her release was granted only upon his giving bonds in a large sum to take her out of the Colony, and even then the authorities stipulated that she should be permitted to speak with no one during the journey. Upon these conditions she was conducted under guard beyond the settlements.

In September, 1659, in company with William Robinson, Marmaduke Stevenson, and Nicholas Davis, Mary again, and this time with full knowledge of the peril of the act, visited Boston for the purpose of testifying against the iniquitous laws in force there, or, as they themselves declared, "to look the bloody laws in the face," and to meet the oppressors of her people, as it were, in their own stronghold.

Short was the time allowed them. The four were quickly made prisoners and brought before the Court, which passed sentence of banishment, with the penalty of death should they return. They were then released, and ordered to depart out of the Colony. Not obeying this mandate, Robinson and Stevenson were soon again apprehended, and were again consigned to prison, where they were used like condemned felons, being chained to the floor of their dungeon. Within a month Mary also became, for the second time, an inmate of the same prison, having been recognized and taken while standing in front of it.

The Whipple House at Ipswich, now the home of the Historical Society

Eastham, where the lighthouse of the dunes guides the seafarer

With Mary came Hope Clifton, also of Rhode Island. The declared purpose of the women was to visit and minister to the Friends then in prison. The settled purpose of the prisoners to defy the law being known to their friends, and no mercy being expected for them, several of these came to Boston in order to assist in the last act of the tragedy. One even brought linen for the sufferers' shrouds. All this imparts a highly dramatic character to the acts of the resolute martyrs.

The three prisoners were brought before the Court of Magistrates. The incorruptible but implacable Governor John Endicott presided. The men keeping their hats on, Endicott ordered the officer to pull them off. He then told the prisoners that neither he nor the other magistrates desired their death, but that the laws must be enforced. All three were condemned to be hanged.

Mrs. Dyer heard her doom pronounced with serene composure, simply saying: "The Lord's will be done!"

"Take her away, Marshal," commanded Endicott.

"I joyfully return to my prison," she rejoined.

On her way back to prison, filled with the exaltation of the Spirit, she said to the marshal, or high-sheriff, who was conducting her, "Indeed, you might let me alone, for I would go to the prison without you."

"I believe you, Mrs. Dyer," the officer replied; "but my orders are to take you there, and I must do as I am commanded."

During the interval of a week between the sentence and the day fixed for its execution, Mrs. Dyer wrote an appeal to the General Court, in which she compares herself with Queen Esther, and her mission with that of the queen to Ahasuerus. It is pervaded throughout by a simple and touching dignity. There is not one craven word in it, or one entreating pardon or expressing a doubt of the righteousness of her own acts. Calmly she rehearses the history of her case, and then concludes her appeal, "in love and the spirit of meekness," to the justice and magnanimity of the Court, which was able to set her free. But her prayer was unanswered.

The renewed and earnest intercession of Mrs. Dyer's husband and son were alike ineffectual; the magistrates remained unmoved. It is said that the son, in the hope of saving her, passed the last night in his mother's cell, beseeching her to abjure, or at least so far to retract her mistaken opinions as to give some chance for hope that the judges might yet relent, and commute her sentence of death to banishment. History has kindly drawn the veil over this scene. All we know is that the mother preferred death to dishonor.

Nor were other efforts wanting to save the condemned prisoners. Suitors able to make themselves heard in the council chamber and the Governor's closet earnestly labored to prevent the consummation of the crime.

On Thursday, the 27th of October, in the morning, according to an ancient custom, the drummers of the trained bands beat their drums up and down the streets, to notify the soldiers to get under arms. This being the time-honored lecture-day, which was also the one usually appointed for holding public executions, as soon as the public worship was over, the drums were again heard, the trained bands assembled and formed in order, and were then marched to the prison. Then the high-sheriff, exhibiting his warrant, called for the bodies of the prisoners by name. Their irons were knocked off by the jailer, and, after tenderly embracing each other, they were led forth to take their places in the ranks of the guard, Mary being placed between the two men who were to suffer with her. A great multitude had assembled to witness these solemn proceedings. The procession then moved, the prisoners on foot, the people pressing closely around them, in order not to lose a word of what they might say, but whenever the condemned attempted to speak, the drummers were ordered to beat their drums, and so drowned the voices in the uproar. One sees here, as always, that every tyranny is afraid of its victims. Hemmed in by armed men, and surrounded by a surging and excited throng, the prisoners walked hand in hand all the way to the scaffold, supporting and comforting each other. The brutal marshal, seeing this, said sneeringly to Mary: "Are you not ashamed, you, to walk thus hand in hand between two young men?"

"No," she replied, "this is to me an hour of the greatest joy I could have in this world."

The party having reached the place of execution, Mary and her fellow sufferers bade each other a last farewell. Robinson first ascended the fatal ladder. While he was predicting a visitation of divine wrath upon his slayers, a harsh voice in the crowd cried out: "Hold thy tongue! Thou art going to die with a lie in thy mouth!"

Stevenson's last words were: "Be it known unto all, this day, that we suffer not as evil-doers, but for conscience' sake."

It was now Mary's turn. Her two dear friends were hanging dead before her eyes. Fearlessly she mounted the fatal ladder and submitted herself to the hangman's hands. She was then pinioned, blindfolded, and the fatal noose placed about her neck. All being then ready, the crowd awaited the last act in breathless suspense, when in the distance a voice was heard crying out, "Stop! She is reprieved!"

The agitation of the spectators is something that we can only faintly conceive. But Mary, it is said, remained calm and unmoved through it all. "Her feet being loosed," says Sewel, "they bade her come down. But she, whose mind was already as it were in heaven, stood still, and said she was there willing to suffer as her brethren did, unless they would annul their wicked law." She was then taken down from the scaffold and re-conducted to prison, where her son, who was anxiously awaiting her return, embraced her as one risen from the dead. Only then she learned that to his importunity with the magistrates she owed her deliverance from the fate of her brethren. The son had saved his mother. The death-sentence had been commuted to banishment, but Mary now received a solemn warning to the effect that the extreme penalty would surely be exacted should she again offend against the majesty of the law. She was then conducted under guard to the Colony frontier, whence she pursued her way home to Rhode Island.

But the old impulse reviving in her in full force, in defiance of the warning thrice repeated, Mary again sought to obtain the crown of martyrdom to which she was foreordained. Burning with fanatical zeal, regardless, too, of the conditions which had procured the remission of her sentence, she deliberately violated the law again. In May, 1660, the unfortunate woman had so little regard for her personal safety as again to come to "the bloody town of Boston." She was soon summoned before the General Court. Swift was the judgment, swift the execution. Endicott, indeed offered her a chance of escape, but her soul was too lofty, her purpose too strongly fixed, to avail herself of a subterfuge to save her life. Endicott conducted her examination. He was as hard as iron, she gentle but undaunted.

"Are you the same Mary Dyer that was here before?" he began.

"I am the same Mary Dyer that was here at the last General Court," she replied.

"Then you own yourself a Quaker, do you not?" said the Governor.

"I own myself to be reproachfully called so."

Then the jailer spoke up and said that Mary was a vagabond.

"I must then repeat the sentence once before pronounced upon you," said Endicott.

Mary quietly rejoined: "That is no more than what thou saidst before."

"True," said Endicott sternly, "but now it is to be executed; therefore prepare yourself for 9 o'clock to-morrow."

Mary then began to speak of her call, when the Governor burst out with: "Away with her! away with her!"

In great anguish of mind, he being wholly ignorant that she meditated this fatal step, her husband wrote to the General Court of Massachusetts, once more imploring its clemency. His entreaties would have moved a stone to pity. But it was now too late. On the first day of June the solemn ceremonies of the previous October

Boston Common, looking toward Beacon Street, where the gilded dome of the State House rises above the trees.

were repeated. The scaffold was erected on Boston Common, and at the appointed hour the marshal came for her. The authorities having reason to fear a popular tumult, caused the prisoner strongly guarded to be taken over a circuitous route to the fatal spot. Once more Mary ascended the scaffold with a firm step. Some of the people made a last effort to save her, but Mary would not agree to leave the country. To the expressed hope that her life might be spared the officer commanding the guard retorted that she was guilty of her own blood.

"Nay," she replied, "I came to keep bloodguiltiness from you, desiring you to repeal the unrighteous and unjust law made against the innocent servants of the Lord."

A colloquy by which her last moments were embittered was kept up on the scaffold. She was reproached for saying she had been in paradise. "Yes," said this undaunted woman, "I have been in paradise several days." The executioner then performed his office.

BOSTON'S JUDGMENT
ON ANN HIBBINS

MRS. ANN HIBBINS, the aged widow of a merchant of note, the reputed sister of the Deputy Governor of the Colony, was tried, convicted and suffered death at Boston in the year 1656 for being a witch. This relationship by blood and marriage announces a person of superior condition in life, and not some wretched and friendless hag such as is associated with the popular idea of a witch. It supposes her to have had connections powerful enough to protect her in such an extremity as that of life or death in which she was placed. But in her case it is clear that they were powerless to stay the final execution of the horrid sentence, which was carried into effect with all its revolting details, according to the decree of the court.

To be censorious is easy here. Such a tale of horror is in fact a shock to all our preconceived notions of the solid wisdom and well-balanced judgments characterizing our ancient lawgivers. Still, when kings wrote learned treatises, ministers preached, and poets rhymed about it — when the penal statutes of all civilized states recognized and punished it as a crime — people of every condition

51

may well be pardoned for putting full faith in witchcraft as a thing belonging to the category of incontestable facts, admitted by the wisest and holiest men, and punished as such by the ordinations of God and man. What is the wonder, then, that they dealt with it as a fact? We may lament their ignorance, but we should be slow to condemn them for being no wiser than their own generation.

This case of Mrs. Hibbins is further interesting as being the second one that the lamentable annals of witchcraft record, that of Margaret Jones, in 1648, being the first. The simple statement should suffice to correct the belief that the Salem outbreak was the beginning, instead of the tragical end, of the delusion in New England. Mrs. Hibbins's cause is also memorable as the first known instance of the General Court of the Colony sitting in trial in a case of life and death. The tragedy, therefore, lacked no element of solemnity to render it deeply impressive.

Mrs. Ann Hibbins was the wife of William Hibbins, a wealthy and influential merchant of Boston. Hutchinson says he was one of the principal merchants in the Colony. He had served the Colony with credit, first as its agent in England, and again as one of the assistants, or chief magistrates. These important trusts denote the high esteem in which he was held, and they confirm his admitted capacity for public affairs. A series of unlucky events, however, brought such heavy losses upon him in his old age as seriously to impair his estate, but what was perhaps worse to bear, the sudden change from affluence to a more straitened way of living is alleged not only to have soured his wife's naturally unstable temper, but to have unsettled her mind, so that she became in turn so morose and so quarrelsome as to render her odious to all her neighbors. Instead of being softened by misfortune, she was hardened and embittered by it. It is thought that some of these neighbors were led to denounce her as a witch through motives of spite, or in revenge for her abusive treatment.

It was a credulous age, when the spirit of persecution was easily aroused. The eye of the whole town was presently turned

A wintry view of a corner of Boston Common, showing the spire of the Park Street Church, where S. F. Smith's *America* was first sung.

upon Mrs. Hibbins. There is little room to doubt that she was the
unfortunate possessor of a sharp tongue and of a crabbed temper.
Most unfortunately for her, a superior intelligence and penetration
enabled her to make shrewd guesses about her neighbors and their
affairs, which the old wives and gossips believed no one but the
devil or his imps could have known. From dislike they advanced to
hatred, then to fear, and then it began to be whispered about that
she was a witch. Such a reputation would naturally cast a fatal
blight over her life. No wife or mother believed herself or her infant for one moment safe from the witch's detestable arts, since she
might take any form she pleased to afflict them. Presently, the idle
gossip of a neighborhood grew into a formal accusation.

The increasing feeling of detestation and fear having now
broken out into a popular clamor for justice upon the witch, Mrs.
Hibbins was first publicly expelled from the communion of her
church, and then publicly accused and thrown into prison. When
the prison door closed behind her, her doom was sealed.

Fortunately her husband had died a year before and was not
alive to meet the terrible accusation or to stem the tide setting so
strongly and so pitilessly against his wife. If her brother, Richard
Bellingham, then holding the second place in the Colony, made
any effort to save her, that fact nowhere appears. Her three sons
were absent from the Colony. Alone, friendless, an object of hatred
to her own neighbors, her heart may well have sunk within her.

Under such distressing circumstances was poor old Dame
Hibbins dragged from her dungeon before the Court which was to
try her as the worst of criminals. The jury, however, failed to con-
vict her of any overt act of witchcraft. But she could not escape
thus. The people, it is said, demanded her blood, and nothing short
of this would satisfy them. So the magistrates, having the power to
set aside the verdict, obeying the popular voice, brought her before
the bar of the General Court, where she was again required to
plead guilty or not guilty to being a witch. She answered with firmness and spirit that she was not guilty, and said she was willing to

be tried by God and the Court. The evidence already taken against her was then read, witnesses were heard, and her answers considered, and the court by its vote found her guilty of witchcraft, according to the tenor of the bill of indictment. Governor Endicott then pronounced the awful sentence of death upon the doomed woman for a crime which had no existence save in the imagination of her accusers. The warrant for her execution was made out in due form, the fatal day was fixed, and the marshal-general was therein directed to take with him "a sufficient guard." Then the poor, infirm, superannuated woman was led back to prison a condemned felon.

As the sentence was not carried into effect for a whole year, it is probable that the intercession of friends procured this reprieve. But it could not avert her final doom. On the day she was to suffer she executed in prison a codicil to her will, disposing of all her property. She was then taken to the usual place of execution and hanged.

The "usual place of execution" being the Common, it is a tradition that Mrs. Hibbins, as well as others who suffered at the hands of the public executioner, was launched into eternity from the branch of the Great Elm Tree that once stood, a commanding and venerated relic of the past, near the center of this beautiful park. Her remains were shamefully violated. A search was immediately made upon the dead body of the poor woman for the distinguishing marks that all witches were supposed to have on their persons. Her chests and boxes were also ransacked for the puppets or images by which the victims of witches were supposed to be afflicted, but none was found. The remains were probably thrust into some obscure hole, for the sufferer, being excommunicated and a condemned witch, would not be entitled to Christian burial, although she earnestly begged this poor boon in her will. And all this really happened in the good town of Boston in the year 1656!

KING CHARLES II
INTERCEDES FOR THE
PERSECUTED QUAKERS

THIS was no common letter that early in November, 1661, fell like a bombshell into the wicked town of Boston. It was certainly an alarming manifesto. It brought a proud and sensitive people, who had ceased to pay respect to loyalty, and had almost forgotten its forms, once more rudely to their knees. And they were a stern race, fearing God more than they honored the King. But they felt the shock that had just overthrown the Puritan Commonwealth; and the voice which rose from among its ruins, commanding them to obey, sounded at the moment in their ears very much like the voice of God. This was the King's message:

CHARLES R.

Trusty and Wellbeloved, we greet you well. Having been informed that several of our subjects among you, called Quakers, have been and are imprisoned by you, whereof some have been executed, and others (as hath been represented unto us) are in danger to undergo the like: We have thought fit to signify our pleasure in that behalf for the future, and do require, that if there be any of those people called Quakers amongst you, now already condemned to suffer death, or other corporal punishment, or that are imprisoned, or obnoxious to the like condemnation, you are to forbear to proceed any farther, but that you forthwith send the said persons (whether condemned or imprisoned) over to this our Kingdom of England, together with their respective crimes or offences laid to their charge, to the end such course may be taken with them here, as shall be agreeable to our laws and their demerits. And for so doing, these our letters shall be your sufficient warrant and discharge. Given at our Court at Whitehall, the 9th day of September, 1661, in the thirteenth year of our reign.

Subscribed, To our Trusty and Wellbeloved John Endicot, Esq.; and to all and every other the Governor or Governors of our plantation of New England, and of the colonies thereunto belonging, that now are, or hereafter shall be: And to all and every the ministers and officers of our said plantation and colonies whatever, within the continent of New England.

By His Majesty's Command.

WIL. MORRIS

Continued encroachment on the prerogative of the throne had doubtless much to do with ordering their destiny, possibly as much as had the cruelties practiced against the offending Quakers, to whose prayers for redress the Parliament had paid little attention. But with the return of the old monarchy, its likings and its hatreds, the politic Friends had hopes that the easy-going Charles would lend a more gracious ear to them in the hour of his great triumph over the Puritan cause. Nor would he be found unwilling to lower the pride of those haughty Puritan subjects on the other side of the Atlantic, who were endeavoring to carry on a little commonwealth of their own. The moment was indeed opportune. Floating in adulation, Charles II was well disposed to clemency toward all except those who had kept him in exile for twelve years. The Quakers on their part were strongly aroused to make renewed efforts by the news of the execution of William Leddra at Boston. Then Edward Burroughs, a leading Friend and a man of action, entreated and obtained an audience of the King.

When he was ushered into the presence-chamber his first words were: "Sire, there is a vein of innocent blood opened in your Majesty's dominions which, if not stopped, may overrun all."

"I will stop that vein," said the King, shortly.

Burroughs then laid before the King a detailed account of what had been done in New England. After he had given the catalogue of scourgings, brandings, cropped ears, banishments upon pain of death, and lastly of the execution of four persons of this sect for presuming to return to the Colony when forbidden to do so, he presented the King with proofs that the New England authorities had refused to allow the Quakers an appeal to England when they had demanded it. His Majesty is reported to have taken great notice of this item of the indictment, calling out to the lords who were with him: "Lo! these are my good subjects of New England."

He then inquired when a ship would be ready to sail for New England, and dismissed Burroughs with the promise that he should presently hear from him through the Lord Chancellor. This promise Charles punctually kept. The mandatory letter was duly prepared under date of September 9, 1661, and then whom should the King's minister select to be the bearer of it, but Samuel Shattuck, an exiled Quaker, who had given the New England magistrates no end of trouble, having been finally banished from the Colony upon pain of death.

The London Friends chartered a vessel, of which Ralph Goldsmith, another Quaker, was captain, to carry the King's order and his messenger to Boston. In six weeks the ship arrived at her destination. It being the Sabbath, all the company remained quietly on board.

Seeing a vessel, with an English ensign at her peak, cast anchor in their road, some of the selectmen of the town hastened on board to learn the news. They eagerly asked the captain if he had brought any letters, for intelligence of the events then taking place in England was awaited with the utmost anxiety and impatience. The master replied that he had, but he would not deliver them on that day; and so his visitors got into their boat and went on shore again as wise as they came. But in the meantime some of them having recognized Shattuck and others on board as being

Quakers, they spread the report that "Shattuck and the devil and all had come back again."

The next morning, armed with the King's mandate, Shattuck came on shore accompanied by Goldsmith, the master, and the two went directly to Governor Endicott's house, passing on the way the market-place where so many of their friends had been mercilessly whipped, and the jail in which so many were still confined. They knew they were bearding the lion when they knocked at the Governor's door. The servant who opened it asked what was their business with his master; they bade him say that, being charged with the commands of his Majesty the King, they should deliver their message into none but the Governor's own hands. They were then admitted without further questioning, and presently the Governor came in to them, but upon perceiving that Shattuck kept his hat on, he commanded it to be taken off, which was done. Then having received the deputation and the papers, the Governor formally acknowledged its official character by removing his own hat, and ordering that of Shattuck to be given to him again. Yet the man who now stood before him, enjoying the Governor's moral degradation while protected by an inviolable safeguard, was the same one whom Endicott formerly had sentenced to stripes and banishment. The draught was a bitter one, but Endicott bore himself with dignity. After this byplay indicating the homage due to royalty and its representative, the Governor read the letter, and bidding Shattuck and Goldsmith to follow him, went to the Deputy Governor's house, and laid the papers before Bellingham. After some conference with the Deputy, the Governor turned to the messengers and said briefly and with dignity: "We shall obey his Majesty's command."

After this interview was ended, Goldsmith gave liberty to all his passengers to come on shore, and afterward they publicly held a religious meeting with those of their faith in the town, "returning thanks to God for his mercy manisfested in this most wonderful deliverance." As all such assemblies as this had been unlawful, this act announced the King's active intervention in their affairs to the people. An order soon after released all Quakers then in custody.

Fishing boats at Gloucester, a busy port for three hundred years

Other boats in Gloucester harbor

CAPE ANN

The great granite headland of Cape Ann gave solid footing to Roger Conant and his little band of adventurers when they landed in 1623. They had been sent by the Rev. John White and others of Dorchester to establish a "plantation for the propagation of religion," but they met such hardships that in two years Conant was "looking out a situation more commodious for a town." White prevailed upon Conant, who, according to Cotton Mather, was "a most religious, prudent, worthy gentleman," to remain on the promise that more friends, goods and provisions would be sent. On March 19, 1627, the Council of Plymouth in England sold a group of Dorchester gentlemen "that part of New England which lies between a great river called Merrimack and a certain other river there called Charles River, in the bottom of Massachusetts Bay." Conant and his men moved down to the harbor of Naumkeag, later called Salem, and a new tide of immigration built permanent settlements on Cape Ann.

Gloucester, Bass Rocks, Magnolia, Annisquam were added to the map. At Rockport men sawed great blocks out of

*the granite base for walls and roads. Here stands the old
pioneer garrison, converted into a dwelling and known as
the Garrison Witch House, because in 1692 it gave shelter
to Elizabeth Proctor, who had stood trial for witchcraft in
Salem, together with her husband, and had been permitted
to go free because of her pregnancy, her husband being executed. Here, in West Gloucester, the suitably-named Hesperus
Avenue leads to Rafe's Chasm, from which the visitor can
discern the reef of Norman's Woe, on which the* Hesperus
was shattered.

B Y COMMAND of Nature, one of those iron-ribbed ridges which
it astounds us to see forests growing and people living upon,
detaches itself from the Essex coast, and advances steadily five
leagues out into the sea. Halting there, it covers its head with a
bristling array of rocky islands and jagged reefs, which, like skir-
mishers in the front of battle, now here, now there, announce
their presence in the offing by puffs of water smoke. An incessant
combat rages between these rocks and the advancing ocean. From
the Highlands, at the land's end, it is possible on a clear day to
make out the dim white streak of Cape Cod stretching its emaciated
arm from the south coast towards this half-extended and rock-
gauntleted one from the north. Between the two capes, which
really seem to belong to different zones, is the entrance to the
grand basin of Massachusetts Bay, over which, in the darkness, the
brilliant rays from Thacher's and Highland lighthouses cross each
other like flaming sword-blades. Among the thousands that have
passed in or out, one seeks in his memory for only one little bark
carrying an entire nation. The *Mayflower* passed here.

The sea welcomes the intruding headland with inhospitable
arms; but at the extreme point, where the rock is pierced and the
sea flows in, there is a port of refuge that became the greatest fish-
ing-mart in the nation. Without regard to season the waters around

THEY THAT GO
DOWN TO THE SEA
IN SHIPS
1623 – 1923

The Bronze Fisherman looks out to the sea at Gloucester

it were covered with a flight of sails entering or leaving the principal port, reminding one of the restless sea-gulls that circle about their rocky aerie.

The muscular shoulder of the Cape is occupied by the towns of Beverly, Wenham, and Hamilton, the central portion by Manchester and Essex, and the extremity by Gloucester and Rockport. Nearly the whole interior region remains the same untamed wilderness that it was a hundred years ago; for among these rugged hills there is little land that is fit for farming, and that little is found in the hollows, or bordering upon occasional arms of the sea. There are, however, extensive and valuable forests of pine and cedar covering scattered portions with a perennial green. The sea having peopled it, and the land offering nothing better than stones, timber, and fuel, the fishing-villages were built close to the edge of the shore, where there were natural harbors like that of Gloucester, or upon tidal creeks or inlets like those of Manchester and Annisquam. From these villages sprang a hardy race of sailors renowned in song and story. One does not think of these people as having any fixed relation with the land: they are amphibious.

The general and apparently irreclaimable sterility of the Cape drove the earliest settlers back upon the mainland. They therefore abandoned their rude cabins and their fishing-stages at the extreme end of the Cape, and newly began what was later on called Salem, which at first included the whole Cape. Yet notwithstanding this desertion, settlements were soon begun at Beverly and Manchester, and Gloucester was permanently re-occupied on account of the excellence and advantageous position of its harbor. But for a time these settlements were very humble ones. Roger Conant says that in his time Beverly was nicknamed Beggarly. He wished to have it changed to Budleigh, after a town in Devonshire, England. He remarks that he had no hand in naming Salem, where he built the first house. Nor were Blackstone, the first white settler of Boston, or Roger Williams, who founded Providence, more fortunate in securing posthumous remembrance.

Cape Ann Historical House, Gloucester →

Bayard Taylor was nevertheless extremely taken with the picturesqueness of the interior of Cape Ann, and he was a traveller who had grown something fastidious in his notions of natural scenery. He speaks of it thus:

"A great charm of the place is the wild wooded scenery of the inland. There are many little valleys, branching and winding as if at random, where the forests of fir and pine, the great, mossy bowlders, the shade and coolness and silence, seem to transfer you at once to the heart of some mountain wilderness. The noise of the sea does not invade them; even the salt odor of the air is smothered by the warm, resinous breath of the pines. Here you find slender brooks, pools spangled with pond-lily blossoms, and marshes all in a tangle with wild flowers. After two or three miles of such scenery there is no greater surprise than to find suddenly a blue far deeper than that of the sky between the tree trunks, and to hear the roar of the breakers a hundred feet below you."

While exploring the coast one finds it continually shifting from beaches of hard sand, strewn with a fine dark gravel, to picturesque coves bordered with rocks shattered into colossal fragments and bulging out like masses that have suddenly cooled, become rusted by spray, worn to glassy smoothness, yet all split and fractured and upheaved by the powerful blows dealt by the waves. These coves make the most charming summer retreats imaginable; and some of them, like Old Kettle Cove, — which under the name of Magnolia has a sweeter sound, — and Pigeon Cove, have turned their primitive solitudes into populousness, and their once worthless rocks into pedestals for the scores of beautiful villas that have sprung up upon their bald and overhanging brows.

In one place, say that you leave the road in order to walk over a smooth esplanade of sand, up whose gentle slope one wave chases another unceasingly, while the forest-trees skirting the head of the beach bend over and watch this fierce play, with all their leaves trembling. You look off over the ridged and sparkling sea-foam into the open mouth of Marblehead Harbor, whose iron headlands the distance softens to forms of wax. Two or three treeless islands are luxuriously dozing in the sun and sea. This must be the haven where the fleet of Winthrop first furled its tattered sails after a tempestuous voyage across the Atlantic of more than two months. Yes, there is Baker's Isle, and there is Little Isle, within which it anchored. Then it was here that the colonists, of whom he was the Moses, first set foot on the soil of their Promised Land, and it was here they roamed among the rocky pastures, gathering wild strawberries and roses, examining everything with eager curiosity, and perhaps with doubt whether it was all real.

Not many years ago, while a guest of the genial and gifted James T. Fields, whose cottage was a conspicuous object on the bald brow of Thunderbolt Hill in Manchester, Bayard Taylor was taken to visit Richard H. Dana, the venerable poet who discovered the genius of Bryant. The poet traveller, obeying the habit of a lifetime, jotted down some minutes of his visit serving to recall the man and the scene to our remembrance. He says:

"Retracing our way a mile or so, we took a different road, and approached the coast through open, grassy fields, beyond which, on the edge of a lofty bluff, stood the gray old mansion of the venerable poet, Richard H. Dana. The place is singularly wild, lonely, and picturesque. No other dwelling is visible. A little bight of the coast thrusts out its iron headlands at a short distance on either side; the surf thunders incessantly below, and in front the open ocean stretches to the sky. Mr. Dana's only neighbors are the vessels that come and go at greater or less distances."

As we approach the end of the Cape we enter a storied region. Here is the deep cleft known as Rafe's Chasm, and the tawny clump of stark ledges which the coast throws off and the sea flies incessantly at, called Norman's Woe. Then we enter the beautiful islet-studded harbor of Gloucester, and with an interest that the natural beauties of the spot enhance, we fix our eyes upon the verdurous southern shore, for here the little colony of Roger Conant, the pioneer governor, maintained a struggling existence, until, like a garrison that can no longer hold out, it fell back to

Eastern Point Light, Gloucester

Salem, newly chose its ground, and again bravely confronted its old enemies, want and neglect. But long before him, this cape in the sea picked up many adventurous *voyageurs*.

In the heart of the Gloucester woodlands a most interesting floral phenomenon exists. There, apparently defying nature's lines and laws, the beautiful magnolia of the South unfolds in secret its snowy flowers and exhales its spicy perfume. Another phenomenon is the beach at Manchester, whose sands emit weird musical tones when crushed by the passage of wheels through them. Still another is the enormous Moving Rock at Squam Common, a heavy mass of granite so exactly poised that the pressure of a child's finger is sufficient to change its position.

This sterile sea-cape may also lay claim to other and more enduring associations than the memories of a summer passed among its rocky sea-nooks can afford. Beverly was the home of Robert Rantoul, whose epitaph has been written by Whittier, and of Lucy Larcom; Hamilton that of Abigail Dodge; Essex, of Rufus Choate; Gloucester, of E. P. Whipple and William Winter. Manchester was Dana's by adoption, as well as the summer haunt of Oliver Wendell Holmes, James Fields, Annie Fields and Elizabeth Phelps. Dr. E. H. Chapin loved his summer home at Pigeon Cove; and it was there he sought relief from the haunting "demon of the study." This was also the favorite haunt of William Cullen Bryant and of Starr King; so that among those who were either native or habitually sojourners are many of the men and women most eminent in our literary annals.

The legends of Cape Ann deal mostly with seafaring, but there is one with quite substantial footing on the land. It is the story of the Spectre Leaguers.

A Colonial cottage in Annisquam on Cape Ann

Gables and dormers at Annisquam on Cape Ann

The Spectre Leaguers of Cape Ann

The fatal year 1692, in which the witchcraft terrorism spread, had one ludicrous chapter to redeem it from utter fatuity.

It is gravely told in the *Magnalia Christi* of Cotton Mather, and on the authority of the Reverend John Emerson of Gloucester, that a number of rollicking apparitions, dressed like gentlemen in white waistcoats and breeches, kept that and the neighboring towns in a state of feverish excitement and alarm for a fortnight. Neither of the reverend persons named seems to have entertained a doubt that these unaccountable molestations were caused by the devil and his agents, who took the human form for the better execution of their deep design. The spectres, if such they were, appear to have been a harmless sort of folk, for they did no injury to the persons or the property of the inhabitants. But the fact that they were spirits, vouched for by such high authority as Cotton Mather, would seem to dispose of doubt on the subject.

In the midsummer of 1692 Ebenezer Babson, a sturdy yeoman of Cape Ann, with the rest of his family, almost every night heard noises as if some persons were walking or running about the house. He being out late one night, when returning home saw two men come out of his own door, and then at sight of him run swiftly from the end of the house into the adjoining cornfield. Going in, he immediately questioned his family concerning these strange visitors. They promptly replied that no one at all had been there during his absence. Staggered by this denial, but being a resolute, stout-hearted man, Babson seized his gun and went out in pursuit of the intruders. When he had gone a little way from the house, he saw the same men suddenly start up from behind a log and run into a swamp nearby. He also overheard one say to the other, "The man of the house is now come, else we might have taken the house." Then he lost sight of them.

Upon this the whole family rose in consternation, and went with all haste to the nearest garrison, which was only a short distance off. They had only just entered it when they heard heavy footfalls, as if a number of men were trampling on the ground around it. Then Babson again took his gun and ran out, and he again saw the two men running down the hill into the swamp. By this time no one doubted that the settlers were threatened with an Indian foray and that these men were the enemy's scouts.

The next night but one, Babson, for the third time, saw two men, who, he thought, looked like Frenchmen, one of them having a bright gun, such as the French Canadians used, slung on his back. Both of them started towards him at the top of their speed, but Babson, taking to his heels, made good his escape into the garrison. When he was safely in, the noise of men moving about on the outside was again distinctly heard. Not long after these strange things had taken place, Babson, with another man named John Brown, saw three men, whom they tried hard to get a shot at, but did not, owing to the strangers' dodging about in so lively a manner that they could not take aim. For two or three nights these men continued to appear in the same mysterious way, for the purpose of drawing the Cape men out into a wild-goose chase after them. On July 14, Babson, Brown, and all the garrison saw within gunshot of them half-a-dozen men, whom they supposed to be reconnoitering, or trying to decoy them into an ambush. The brave garrison at once sallied out in hot pursuit. Babson presently overtook two of the skulking vagabonds, took good aim, and pulled the trigger; but his trusty gun missed fire, and the men got away and hid themselves among the bushes. He then called out to his comrades, who immediately answered, "Here they are! here they are!" when Babson, running to meet them, saw three men stealing out of the swamp side by side. Bringing his gun to his shoulder, with sure aim this time he fired; when all three fell as if shot.

Almost beside himself, Babson cried out to his companions that he had killed three. But when he had come nearly up to the supposedly dead men, they rose up and ran away, apparently without hurt or wound. Indeed one of them gave Babson a shot in re-

Along the docks at Rockport

A peaceful estuary at Lanesville

turn for his own, the bullet narrowly missing him, and burying itself in a tree, from which it was afterward dug out, and preserved as a trophy of the combat. Babson thinking this warm work, took refuge behind a tree and reloaded. Then, his comrades having joined him, they all charged together upon the spot where the fugitives lay concealed. Again the spectres started up before their eyes and ran, "every man his way." One, however, they surrounded and hemmed in, and Babson, getting a fair shot at him, saw him drop. But when search was made, the body had vanished. After a fruitless hunt, during which the stout-hearted Colonists heard loud talking in the swamp, they returned, half dead with fatigue, to the garrison. But no sooner were they back there, than they saw more men, who prudently kept out of gunshot. What could it all mean?

The next morning Babson started for the harbor in order to give the alarm, for it was not doubted by any one that an attack was imminent. While on his way he was waylaid and fired at by the "unaccountable troublers," who, strange to say, loaded their guns with real bullets, as poor Babson was near finding out to his cost. Having procured help, the neighborhood was scoured for traces of the attacking party, two of whom were seen, but not being mortal flesh and blood, could not be harmed by lead or steel.

In the course of a few days more, two of the garrison went out upon a scout, and saw several men come out of an orchard, in which they seemed to be performing some strange incantations. They counted eleven of them. Richard Dolliver raised his gun and fired into the midst of them, where they stood the thickest, but of course without other effect than to make them scatter as before.

It now being clear that the strange visitors bore a charmed life, and that the Cape was in great peril from this diabolical invasion, the aid of the surrounding towns was invoked. A reinforcement of sixty men from Ipswich, coming promptly to the rescue, gave the garrison much encouragement. For a fortnight they had been kept in continual alarm, night and day. The infernal visitants showed themselves first in one place and then in another, until a foeman seemed lurking in every bush. Though repeatedly shot at, none could be killed. They threw stones, beat upon barns with clubs, and otherwise acted more in the spirit of diabolical revelry than as if actuated by any deadlier purpose. They moved about the swamps without leaving any tracks. In short, it was evident that such adversaries must be fought with other weapons besides match-locks and broadswords; consequently a strange fear fell upon the Cape.

Finally the strangers became still more bold, and far from taking to their heels when they were chased, they now treated their pursuers with open contempt. For instance, seeing three of the un-known approaching him one morning, walking slowly and ap-parently unmindful of any danger, Babson esconced himself behind some bushes to lie in wait for them. He held his fire until they were come within a stone's throw before he pulled the trigger. But to his unspeakable dismay his gun flashed in the pan, though he repeatedly snapped it at the phantoms, who took no other notice of him than to give him a disdainful look as they walked by. Yet he soon afterward snapped the same gun several times in succes-sion, and it never once missed fire.

It being settled that these insults proceeded from spectres, and not from beings vulnerable to weapons of mortal make, the un-equal contest was abandoned. When this was done, the demons' occupation gone, they disappeared.

It should be said that the most conservative minds regarded these occurrences as part of a descent from the invisible world, which they looked upon as threatening the churches and the peace of the Colony.

Old Meg, The Witch of Gloucester

There was a reputed witch by the name of Margaret Wesson, and familiarly known by the name of Old Meg, who once resided in Gloucester. After having been for many years the object of superstitious curiosity and dread to the inhabitants of the Cape, she at length came to her end in the following strange and mysterious manner.

At the time of the celebrated victorious siege of Louisburg by the Colonial troops in 1745, two soldiers of the Massachusetts line belonging to Gloucester happened to have their attention drawn to the movements of a crow that kept hovering over them. They threw stones, and then fired their muskets at it, but could neither touch nor terrify it; the bird still continued flying round them and cawing horribly in their ears. At length it occurred to one of them that it might be Old Meg. He communicated his suspicions to his comrade; and as nothing but silver was believed to have any power to injure a witch, they cut the silver buttons from their uniform coats and discharged them at the crow. The experiment succeeded. At the first shot they broke its leg; at the second it fell dead at their feet.

When they returned to Gloucester, they learned that Old Meg had broken her leg while walking by the fort in that place at the precise time when they had shot and killed the crow five hundred miles distant; after lingering for a while in great agony she died. And now comes the singular part of the story; upon examining her fractured limb, the identical silver buttons which the soldiers had fired from their muskets under the walls of Louisburg were extracted from the flesh.

The story of Old Meg was long familiarly told in Gloucester, although the credulity which once received it as solemn truth has nearly, if not quite, passed away, according to the Reverend Charles W. Upham, who made this statement in 1832. It has, however, been reproduced among the sober records of fact contained in Babson's *History of Gloucester.*

IPSWICH LEGENDS

OLD IPSWICH is one of the most delightful corners into which the artist or the antiquary could have the good fortune to stray, for here either will find abundant occupation. Its physiognomy is old, its atmosphere drowsy, its quiet unbroken. The best residences are still the oldest ones, and among them are some very quaint specimens of the early Colonial architecture, upon which time seems to have made little impression; while here and there others stand up mere crazy hulks, so shaken and dilapidated inside and out, that every gale threatens to bring them down with a loud crash into the cellars beneath. Some of these have the reputation of being haunted houses, and are of course enveloped in mystery, — and indeed the whole atmosphere of the place is thick with legendary lore, which the old people drop their voices when they are relating.

To me there is no more striking picture than that of some crazy old structure, trembling, as the wind shakes it, like an old man with the palsy, its windows gaping wide, its chimney bent and tottering, the fire on its hearthstone extinguished forever, the path

A habitation for three hundred years — the Emerson-Howard House at Ipswich

An expansive Colonial mansion in Ipswich

An ancient house in Ipswich

Undisturbed boat haven at Ipswich

to it overgrown with weeds, the old well choked up with rubbish and poisonous ivy, — everything expressing irretrievable decay, — standing in the midst of a still vigorous orchard just putting forth its sweet perennial bloom, with the fresh and tender grass creeping up to the broken threshold, as if Nature claimed admittance, and would not be much longer denied. That house, you are told, was built two centuries ago. Where are the builders; and where the generations that came after them? The old well-sweep creaks mournfully in the wind, and points its bony finger to the sky. Yet here are the trees that they planted, still putting forth their buds, like mortals putting on immortality.

It is natural, I think, in such a place to try to imagine the first-comers looking about them. How did it look; what did they think? They were a mere handful, — the apostolic number, — a vanguard sent to establish a semi-military post. Upon ascending the hill above the river they found an outcropping ledge of goodly extent, forming a sort of natural platform, and upon this rock they built their church, which subsequently became so famous throughout the Colony under the successive ministrations of Ward, Rogers, Norton, and Hubbard, all men eminent for their learning and piety. Satan himself was not able to prevail against it; for upon the smooth ledge outside is still seen the distinct print of his sable majesty's cloven foot, when he was hurled from the pinnacle to the ground for attempting to conceal himself within the sanctuary.

In another place, down by the river side, the house where Harry Main lived is pointed out to the visitor. He having thus a local habitation, the legend concerning him is no vagabond tradition. Harry Main is the Wandering Jew of Ipswich, around whom darkly hangs the shadow of an unpardonable crime and its fearful doom. It is said that he had been by turns a pirate, a smuggler, and a wrecker, who followed the wicked trade of building fires on the sands, in order to decoy vessels among the breakers, where they were wrecked, and their crews perished miserably. For these crimes, at his death he was doomed to be chained on Ipswich Bar, the scene of his former murderous exploits, and everlastingly to coil a cable of sand there. When the cable broke, his demoniacal yells of baffled rage could be heard for miles around; and when those fearful sounds announced the rising gale, mothers would clasp their babes to their breasts, while the men shook their heads and said, "Old Harry's growling again!" His name was long the bugbear used to frighten refractory children into obedience, while the rote on the bar, heard in storms, still audibly perpetuates the legend, with its roar.

The old people living on Plum Island used to say that Harry Main's ghost troubled them by wandering about the sand-hills on stormy nights, so that they were afraid to venture out of doors after dark. Indeed the town itself, in its palmy days, was so full of ghostly legends, that certain localities supposed to be haunted, were scrupulously avoided by the timid ones, who had a mortal dread of being accosted by some vagabond spectre with its tale of horror.

Harry Main's house was ransacked, and every rod of the garden dug up for the money he was supposed to have buried there; but nothing rewarded the search. One good man dreamed three nights in succession that vast sums were buried in a certain hill in the town. He could see the very spot. Haunted by the realism of the dream, he determined to test the matter for himself; and one dark night, just as midnight struck, he took his spade, his lantern, and his Bible, and started on his weird errand. Upon reaching the spot he recognized it as the same that he had seen in his dream. He immediately fell to work. After plying his spade vigorously a while, it struck against some hard object. Scraping the earth away with feverish haste, he came to a flat stone having a bar of iron laid across it. This he eagerly grasped with one hand, and was about to turn the stone over with the other when he was suddenly surrounded by a troop of cats, whose eyeballs blazed in the darkness. The digger felt his hair slowly rising on end. A cold sweat stood on his brow. Brandishing the bar aloft, he cried out, "Scat!" when these vigilant guardians of the treasure vanished in a twinkling, leaving the crestfallen money-digger standing up to his middle in cold water, which had poured into the hole, when he broke the spell by speaking. Half drowned, and wholly disgusted, he crawled out of it. The iron bar, however, remained tightly clutched in his hand. He carried it home, and I was assured that upon going to a certain house in Ipswich I might see the identical door-latch which a smith had made out of this bar for a souvenir of the night's adventure.

Ipswich cottages in a winter setting

MARBLEHEAD

ONE HUNDRED YEARS AGO

N EXT TO SWAMPSCOTT comes Marblehead. Quaintest and formerly the most dilapidated of seaports, one can hardly knock
at any door without encountering a legend or a history. Yet the
atmosphere is not oppressive, nor are the suggestions ghostly.

Thanks to fortuitous causes, Marblehead retains more of the
characteristic flavor of the past than any town in New England.
And here one can revel in its memories unchecked, seeing so little
to remind him of the present. Look at the great body of old houses
still composing it! There is no mistaking the era to which they belong. Once among them, one takes a long stride backward into
another century, and is even doubtful if he should stop there. They
are as antiquated as the garments our great-grandfathers wore, and
as little in accord with modern ideas; and yet they were very com-
fortable dwellings in their day, and have even now a home-like
look of solid, though unpretending, thrift. They in fact indicate a
republic of equality, if not one of high social or intellectual refinement. We expect to see sailors in pigtails, citizens in periwigs, and
women in kerchiefs and hobnail shoes, all speaking an unintel-

ligible jargon, and all laying violent tongues on the King's English. We are conscious of a certain incongruity between ourselves and this democracy, which is not at all disagreeable to us, nor disparaging to that.

They have covered a bare and uncouth cluster of gray ledges with houses, and called it Marblehead. These ledges stick out everywhere; there is not enough soil to cover them decently. The original gullies intersecting these ledges were turned into thoroughfares, which meander about after a most lawless and inscrutable fashion. The principal graveyard is situated on the top of a rocky hill, where the dead mariners might lie within sound of the sea they loved so well. And we learn that it was chosen because it was a "sightly place." But in general the dead fare no better than the living, they

Old Burying Ground on Marblehead Hill

Marblehead skyline in winter from Crocker Park

being tucked away in odd corners, here on a hill-top, there in a hollow, the headstones seeming always a part of the ledges above which they rise in straggling groups, stark, gray, and bent with age, intensifying a thousand-fold the pervading feeling of sadness and loneliness associated with such places.

One street carries us along with the present; the other whisks us back into the past again. We dive into a lane, and bring up in a blind alley without egress. Does any one know the way here, we question? We see a crooked crack separating rows of houses, and then read on a signboard that it is such or such a street. In an hour we look upon the whole topography of the place as a jest.

Now and then the mansion of some Colonial nabob — perhaps a colonel or a magistrate — has secured for itself a little breathing space; but in general the houses crowd upon and elbow each other in "most admired disorder." The wonder is that they built here at all, the site was so unpromising; but the harbor was good, there was room to dry fish, and the sailor-settlers looked upon

Looking down Summer Street, Marblehead. *Right*, the Old Town House amid Colonial setting in Marblehead

the sea, and not the shore, as being their home. So that Allerton's rough fellows, who in 1633 made their rude cabins on the harbor's edge, were not looking for farms, but for codfish.

After looking over the town a while, one comes to the conclusion that the first-comers must have tossed up coppers for the choice of building lots, and then made their selection regardless of surveyor's lines. As a consequence, Marblehead is picturesque, but bewildering. It has a placid little harbor, indented by miniature coves, lighted by a diminutive lighthouse, and defended by a dismantled fortress without a garrison. Blindfold a stranger, bring him to Marblehead, and then remove the bandage, and he will certainly exclaim, "This is in the Orkneys, or the Hebrides!"

It is probable that no other spot of ground in the Colonies was so peculiarly adapted to the growth of the marvellous as this. The men, and the boys too, as soon as they were able to handle an oar,

The Old Powder House at Marblehead. *Right*, a vista of Old North Church, Marblehead

followed the sea, while the women did most of the shore work, taking care of and curing the fish. So that in the fishing season the place was nearly as destitute of men as the fabulous island that Peter Martyr tells about in his wonderful *Decades*. The Reverend John Barnard, the patriarch and good genius of the place, tells us that when he first went to Marblehead there was no such thing as a proper carpenter, or mason, or tailor, or butcher in the place; all were fishermen. And this was seventy or eighty years after settlement began here. For half a century there was no settled minister; and for about the same term of years no schoolmaster. To this day no one knows the antecedents of these fishermen, or whence they came. Certain it is that they were no part of the Puritan emigration around them; all accounts agree in styling them a rude, ignorant, lawless, and profligate set, squandering with habitual recklessness the gains of each hazardous voyage. Notorious pirates openly walked the streets; smuggling was carried on like any legitimate occupation. In a word, a community going back to as early a day as any here grew up in the same way that the fishing-stations of Newfoundland gradually turned into permanent settlements, having almost no law and even less religion, until a missionary appeared in the person of the Reverend John Barnard.

As for the women, when we read that on a certain Sabbath-day two hostile Indians, then held as prisoners in the town, were "by the women of Marblehead, as they came out of the meeting-house," tumultuously set upon and barbarously murdered, one easily imagines what the men were like — and the children too, of whom it is soberly said that they were as profane as their fathers. When a stranger appeared in the streets they were in the habit of pelting him with stones. All this prepares us for the appearance of John and Mary Dimond as the legitimate outgrowth of such a

From Colonial days and as good as new, Marblehead

House of Parson John Barnard, Marblehead

place, and for those singular customs, and the still more singular speech, which two centuries could not wholly eradicate. Marblehead, it is quite clear, was not part of the Puritan Commonwealth in any strict sense of the term. It was and is unique.

To illustrate this state of society, let us give one or two examples of old superstitions in order to place the reader in accord with the spirit of those times.

The belief that it is a good omen to see the new moon over one's right shoulder is still universal. Yet this is merely a relic of ancient superstition, although few, perhaps, would be willing to admit that it had any influence upon their future welfare. But our forefathers thought otherwise. Among the early chronicles of Lynn is one giving an account of "an honest old man" who, "as it began to be darkish," went out to look for the new moon, when he espied in the west a strange black cloud, in which presently appeared a

Winter's garlands on Summer Street, Marblehead

complete man-at-arms, standing with his legs a little apart, and holding his pike thrown across his breast in a most martial attitude. The man then called his wife and others to behold this marvel. After a while the man in the cloud vanished; but he was immediately succeeded by the apparition of a stately ship under full sail, although she remained stationary in the heavens. "This," in the words of the narrative, "was seen for a great space, both by these and others of ye same town."

The good old English custom of saluting the new moon had its counterpart in Marblehead, where, on the nights when a new moon was to appear, the unmarried young women would congregate at some houses in the neighborhood for the purpose of having a peep into futurity; and after hanging a huge pot of tallow on the crane over the blazing logs, would then drop, one by one, iron hob-nails into the boiling fat, in the firm belief that the young man who entered while this charm was working would inevitably be the future husband of the fair one who dropped the nails.

At other times the young woman who had a longing to pry into the unknown would go to an upper window of the house and throw a ball of yarn into the street, in the belief that the youth who first picked it up was the man she would marry. All the terrors of the laws against magic could not prevent women from trying the efficacy of magical art in elucidating what to them was the most interesting of all questions. In those times a wedding was a season of unrestrained merrymaking for a whole week. Little ceremony was used. Everybody who chose might attend, and when the guests were ready to depart, the bride and groom were put to bed, and the entire company, regardless of the blushes or screams of the bride, marched round the nuptial couch, throwing old shoes, stockings, and other missiles of established potency, at the newly-wedded couple, by way of bringing them good luck.

Franklin Street, Marblehead

"Stories of phantom ships seen at sea before the loss of a vessel, of the appearance on the water of loved ones who had died at home, of footsteps and voices heard mysteriously in the still hours of the night and coming as warnings from another world, of signs and omens which foretold the approaching death of some member of the family, or prophecies whispered by the winds, that those who were away on the mighty deep would find a watery grave," were interwoven with, and allowed to have an active influence upon, the lives of these people.

The witch of Marblehead was an old crone known and feared as "Mammy Redd, the witch." This woman was believed to possess the power of malignant touch and sight, and she was able, so it was whispered, to cast a spell over those whom she might in her malevolence wish to injure. To some she sent sickness and death, by merely wishing that a "bloody cleaver" might be found in the cradle of their infant children. Upon others she vented her spite by visiting them with petty annoyances. She could curdle milk as it came fresh from the cow's udders, or presently change it into "blue wool," which we take to be another name for blue mould. She was tried and convicted, chiefly on old wives' gabble, and expiated on the gallows the evil fame that she had acquired.

To this fact of history, in which the actors appear testifying under oath to their own superstitious beliefs, we may now add one of those local legends undoubtedly growing out of the frequent intercourse with the free rovers of the main. Among these free-booters it was a law, the cruel policy of which is obvious, that every woman who might become their prisoner should suffer death. The legend is perhaps no more than the echo of one of these tragedies.

It was said that during the latter part of the seventeenth century, a Spanish ship laden with rich merchandise was captured by pirates, who brought their prize into the harbor of Marblehead. The crew and every person on board the ill-fated ship had been butchered in cold blood at the time of the capture, except a beautiful English lady, whom the ruffians brought on shore near what is now called Oakum Bay, and there, under cover of the night, most barbarously murdered her. The few fishermen who inhabited the place were then absent, and the women and children who remained, could do nothing to prevent the consummation of the fearful crime. The piercing screams of the victim were most appalling, and her cries of "Lord, save me! Mercy! O Lord Jesus, save me!" were distinctly heard in the silence of the night. The body was buried on the spot where the deed was perpetrated, and for over one hundred and fifty years, on each anniversary of that dreadful tragedy, the heartening screams of the murdered woman for mercy were said to have been repeated in a voice so shrill and unearthly as to freeze the blood of those who heard them.

Skipper Ireson's Ride

One of the most spirited of John Greenleaf Whittier's home ballads is his *Skipper Ireson's Ride*, which introduced by way of refrain the archaic Marblehead dialect that is now nearly, if not quite extinct. Like most of this poet's characters Skipper Ireson is a real person, whose story, briefly told, is this:

Late in the autumn of the year 1808 the schooner *Betsy* of Marblehead, Benjamin Ireson master, while buffeting its way toward the home port in the teeth of a tremendous gale, fell in with a wreck drifting at the mercy of the winds and waves. This was the schooner *Active*, of Portland, which had been overset in the gale. It was then midnight, with a tremendous sea running. The skipper of the sinking vessel hailed the *Betsy* and asked to be taken off the wreck, from which every wave threatened to wash the distressed and exhausted crew. To this it is said that the *Betsy's* crew strongly demurred, alleging the danger of making the attempt in such a sea in support of their cowardly purpose to abandon the sinking craft to her fate. Some say that Captain Ireson himself was disposed to act with humanity, and to lie by the wreck until daylight, but that he was overruled by the unanimous voice of his men, who selfishly decided not to risk their own miserable lives in order to save others.

The *Betsy's* course was accordingly shaped for Marblehead, where she arrived on the following Sunday. Her crew at once spread the news through the town of their having fallen in with a vessel foundering in the bay, when the Marblehead people, to their honor, immediately despatched two vessels to her relief. But the *Active* had then gone to the bottom of the sea, and the relieving vessels returned from a fruitless search, only to increase the resentment already felt against Skipper Ireson, upon whom his crew had thrown all the blame of their own dastardly conduct.

Town landing, Marblehead

Old Fort Sewall on the headland, Marblehead

Usually dead men tell no tales; but in this instance a more damning evidence of Ireson's inhumanity appeared, as it were, from the grave itself to confront him. On the morning following the night of the *Betsy's* desertion of them, the captain and three others had been rescued from the sinking vessel. They made public the story of the cruel conduct of the *Betsy's* people; and as ill news travels fast, it was not long before it reached Marblehead. Here angered citizens determined to take vengeance on the offender. One moonlight night Skipper Ireson heard a knock at his door. On opening it he found himself in the grasp of a band of resolute men, who silently hurried him off into a deserted place, with what object his fears alone could divine. They first securely pinioned him, and then besmeared him from head to foot with a coat of tar and feathers. In the morning the whole population of the town turned out to witness or assist in this ignominious punishment, which had been planned by some of the bolder spirits, and silently approved by the more timid ones. Ireson in his filthy disguise was seated in the bottom of a dory instead of a cart, and, surrounded by a hooting rabble, dragged through the streets as far as the Salem line. Here the crowd was met and stopped by the selectmen of Salem, who forbade their proceeding farther, thus frustrating their original purpose to drag Ireson through the streets of Salem and Beverly, as well as Marblehead.

During Ireson's rough ride the bottom of the dory had fallen out. The mob then procured a cart, and lifting the boat, culprit and all, upon it, took Ireson back to Marblehead in this way. More dead than alive, he was at last released from the hands of his tormentors and allowed to go home. When he was free, Ireson quietly said to them: "I thank you, gentlemen, for my ride; but you will live to regret it."

Whittier, using the facts as they came to him, and with the sanction of what was in its own time very generally applauded as the righteous judgment of the people of Marblehead, put Ireson in a perpetual pillory, from which no sober second thought is able to rescue him. But whether culpable or not in intention, Ireson's weakness in yielding to his dastard crew, if in fact he did yield, amounted to a grave fault, closely verging upon the criminal. To-day everybody defends Ireson's memory from the charge once as universally believed to be true, when the public verdict was, "served him right." Unfortunately, however, for him, his exasperated townsfolk executed justice on the spot, according to their own rude notions of it, before their wrath had had time to grow cool. But to this fact we owe the most idiosyncratic ballad of purely home origin in the language, although it is one for which the people of Marblehead never forgave the poet.

A MARBLEHEAD LOVE STORY

The austerities of life in Puritan New England did not wipe out the love of a title. The love story of an aristocrat for a poor maid flourished there as in more prosperous lands. It was described often by the popular writers of the eighteenth and nineteenth centuries and was not always the product of fancy. The episode of Agnes and Henry Frankland belongs to the legends of Marblehead, but its outcome is based on a natural catastrophe that made a deep impression on eighteenth century writers — the Lisbon earthquake. In its present form by Drake the legend reflects the sentimental attitude of its period. It invites conjecture of how a writer of the twentieth century would have described Sir Henry's belated chivalry.

THIS PRETTY story, a romance of real life, makes us acquainted with two noble, but impulsive natures, whose destinies first became interwoven in a way quite the reverse of the romantic. After perusing it one is apt to think that this poor Marblehead maiden, this outcast whose great love, finally triumphing over pride, prejudice, suffering, cruel scorn, and every other moral impediment that the world puts in the way of duty, really confers honor upon the noble knight who at last gives her his name, by awakening in him truly ennobling and elevating sentiments. In such a life as that of Agnes one cannot help seeing a design. Without her Sir Henry was a mere votary of pleasure, a man of the world. She really made a man of him at last.

In the summer of 1742 the course of official duty called the Collector of Boston to Marblehead. The incumbent of this office, which had been established with much opposition in the Colonial capital, and was little respected outside of it, was then Henry Frankland, of Mattersea, in Nottinghamshire, who was also connected with one of the greatest families in the North, and who was the heir presumptive to a baronetcy. This young man, who at the early age of twenty-six had come into the possession both of a fortune and of a highly lucrative and honorable appointment, was now in the pursuit of a career. With rank, wealth, and high social position as his birthright, with rare personal attractions, Henry Frankland's future bid fair to become unusually brilliant.

As Marblehead at this period was the smuggling port for Boston, it is quite probable that the Collector's visit, though referred to other causes, looked to the repression of this contraband trade, by which the King's revenues were defrauded and the laws of the realm openly violated.

Henry Frankland, having alighted at the Fountain Inn, found an unexpected obstacle in his path. This was a young and remarkably beautiful girl, who was busily engaged in scrubbing the floor when he entered, and who, we are willing to affirm, found the time to dart an investigating and appreciative glance at the handsome young guest, to whom her own mean garb and menial occupation offered the strongest possible contrast. Struck with the rare beauty of her face and person, the young man stopped to look and to admire. His was the pride of birth and station; hers the submissive deference that the poor and lowly paid to its demands. He was booted and spurred, and wore his laced beaver; she bareheaded and barefooted and on her knees. He had the air of distinction and breeding of his class; she was scrubbing the floor.

The young man called her to him, put some questions negligently, and then, pleased with her answers, dropped a piece of silver into her hand and passed on. He had seen a pretty serving-maid who told him that she was called Agnes — Agnes Surriage. Later a second visit to the inn showed him the same charming picture. Agnes was still doing the drudgery of the inn without shoes or stockings to cover her feet.

When the young man asked why she had not bought them with the money he had given her, she answered that she had indeed done so, but kept them to wear in meeting. Perhaps this elegant young man had unwittingly awakened in her breast, — the painful discovery of a deficiency of which she had been unconscious.

Just what was Henry's first design, or what the workings of his mind, do not at this moment clearly appear; be that as it may, his growing interest in Agnes presently led him to seek an interview with her parents, who were poor and worthy people, and to propose removing their daughter to his own home, in order — Jesuit that he was! — to give her the advantages to which her graces of mind and person, as he warmly protested, fully entitled her. The parents acceded only too readily to the seductive proposal. They could see no danger, not they! Agnes left her own humble home for that of Sir Henry; and so this girl of sixteen became the ward of this grave young gentleman of twenty-six. But, ignorant as she was, and humble and artless, it is easy to believe that she had already taught him something he was in no haste to unlearn.

Agnes did ample justice to her guardian's high opinion of her mental qualifications. The virgin soil is deep and productive. She was taught the commoner branches, as well as the accomplishments then deemed indispensably requisite to the education of a gentle-woman moving in her adopted sphere. As her mind expanded, so did her beauty become more radiant with the consciousness of the new life opening to her. She was a being created to love and be loved. Her gratitude, her confidence, her admiration were all centered upon one object. One day she awoke to the knowledge that she was beloved, and that she loved.

By the death of his uncle, the baronetcy that was hereditary in the Yorkshire branch of the Franklands devolved upon Agnes' guardian, who, having now legitimately inherited it, publicly assumed the title.

The discovery had its usual consequences. Sir Henry Frankland, Baronet, could not dream of laying his noble name at the feet of a serving-maid; not he. His horror of a misalliance was even greater than his abhorrence of a different and a more equivocal connection. But he could not give her up. We will let the veil fall upon the weakness of both of these lovers. He was her idol, she his infatuation; he loved like a man, and she like a woman.

Sir Henry's conduct in openly living with his lovely ward outside of the pale of matrimony being whispered about, was an offence too flagrant for the stern morality of the city of the Puritans to endure; and its indignation was soon made manifest in a way to cut a proud and sensitive nature to the quick. Society he found has its weapons, and can use them, too, without mercy. Society could not justify his leading the girl astray; but it would have forgiven him now, had he chosen to desert her. Boston was no longer a place for Agnes or for him; so that no sooner was he established in his Eden, than an inexorable voice drove him forth. He purchased an estate and built an elegant mansion in the pleasant and secluded inland village of Hopkinton, to which he conveyed Agnes, and with her took up his residence there. While they lived here, the hospitality and luxury of the great house, and the beauty of Sir Henry's companion, were talked about in the country round. Sir Henry devoted himself to the care and embellishment of his estate with the English gentleman's hereditary taste and method. His devotion to Agnes appears to have suffered no diminution; and when at length he was compelled at the call of urgent affairs to visit England, she accompanied him. It is said that he had the hardihood to introduce her among his aristocratic relatives as Lady Frankland. But that ill-advised proceeding met with the repulse it deserved. Throughout all this singular history shines the one ray of hope for Agnes. Except in name, the lovers held unswerving faith to and in each other as completely as if they had been man and wife.

Sir Henry's affairs called him to Lisbon and Agnes went with him. While they were in the Portuguese capital, the dreadful earthquake of 1755 laid the city in ruins. Under these ruins sixty thousand of the inhabitants were buried; the rest fled in terror. The carriage in which Sir Henry happened to be riding was crushed by falling walls, and buried underneath the rubble. Agnes had remained behind and to this accident owed her escape. Running into the street at the first alarm, she avoided death; she was saved, but where was her lord and protector? Frantic and despairing, she followed such faint traces as could be obtained, until chance led her to the spot where Sir Henry lay helpless. A fine lady would have recoiled and fainted dead away; Agnes Surriage, again the working girl of Marblehead, instantly set to work to rescue her lover from the ruins with her own hands. In an hour he was extricated. He was still living. She conveyed him to a place that had escaped the shock of the earthquake, where she nursed him back into health and strength. Vanquished by this last supreme proof of her love for him, the knight gave her his hand in return for his life. And who can doubt that with this act there came back to both that peace of mind which alone was wanting to a perfect union of two noble and loving hearts?

The rockbound
New England Coast

SWAMPSCOTT BEACH

SWAMPSCOTT is a succession of hard sand-beaches and rocky, picturesque headlands, forming with Nahant, Nahant Bay. It was formerly a part of Lynn, and so closely are they united to-day, that it would require a surveyor to tell where the one ends or the other begins. In making a tour of the shores one crosses successively King's Beach, Whale Beach, and Phillips Beach, all of which are the summer playground of the multitudes who come here for health or recreation. The high and glittering shore sweeps gracefully toward the east, far out into the ocean, until it is frittered

away in a cluster of foam-crested ledges that lie in treacherous ambuscade at its extreme point. That curving shore is Phillips Point, and the reef is Dread Ledge. There is a handsome villa or cottage for every elevated site along the two miles of shore.

The extremity of Phillips Point is a wicked-looking shore, and Dread Ledge is the synonym for danger to the mariner. The surrounding waters are thickly sown with half-submerged rocks, which in the delirium of a gale seem rooted in hell itself. Here, in January, 1857, the ill-fated *Tedesco* was swallowed up, with every soul on board. In that memorable gale the sea inundated the marshes, swept unchecked over its ordinary barriers, and heaped a rampart of frozen surf upon the beaches, in which the broken masts of wrecks were left sticking. Streets and roads were so blocked by immense snowdrifts that all travel was suspended for several days. The ponderous anchors of the *Tedesco* were found lying on the top of a rock, and they were all that was left to tell the tale, for not a vestige of the hull remained. Another vessel was afterward wrecked here, but, being driven nearer the land, her crew, one by one, walked to the shore over the bowsprit.

Swampscott was a typical New-England fishing-village. The summer visitors were mere birds of passage, but the men who were native there pursued their hazardous calling the whole year through.

There is no difficulty whatever in placing the scene of Hawthorne's *Village Uncle* here. That sketch is only a series of pictures of the surroundings and of the plain fisherfolk, taken from life, to which, from the snug chimney-corner of a fisherman's humble cottage, the garrulous old Uncle adds his own store of gossip and sea-lore. Hear him:

"Toss on an armful of those dry oak-chips, — the last relics of the 'Mermaid's' knee-timbers, the bones of your namesake, Susan. Higher yet, and clearer, be the blaze, till our cottage windows glow the ruddiest in the village, and the light of our household mirth flash far across the bay to Nahant.

"Now, Susan, for a sober picture of our village! It was a small collection of dwellings that seemed to have been cast up by the sea, with the rock-weed and marine plants that it vomits after a storm, or to have come ashore among the pipe-staves and other lumber which had been washed from the deck of an Eastern schooner. There was just space for the narrow and sandy street between the beach in front and a precipitous hill that lifted its rocky forehead in the rear, among a waste of juniper-bushes and the wild growth of a broken pasture. The village was picturesque in the variety of its edifices, though all were rude. Here stood a little old hovel, built perhaps of driftwood; there a row of boat-houses; and beyond them a two-story dwelling of dark and weatherbeaten aspect, — the whole intermixed with one or two snug cottages painted white, a sufficiency of pigsties, and a shoe-maker's shop."

NEWBURYPORT LEGENDS

U PON LEAVING Ipswich the landscape grows less austere. The flat Rowley marshes succeed the rocky pastures and tumbling hills, with their stiffly-upright cedars and their shut-in vistas, like a calm after a storm. Then we glide on among haycocks, standing up out of the inflowing tide, across the beautiful and peaceful prairie of Old Newbury, and are suddenly brought up by a ridge of high land, lifting its green wall between us and the basin of the Merrimack. At the right, thrust up through the tops of the elm-trees that hide the village, like a spear tipped with gold, "springs the village spire with the crest of its cock in the sun afire."

That is old Newbury meeting-house. Extending far along the slopes of the ridge are the city cemeteries, whose mingled gray and white monuments throng the green swells, a multitude of spectators turned into stone. Then, cutting through the ridge, the train plunges into the darkness of a tunnel, soon emerging again upon the farther slope among the city streets from which the broad white sheet of the Merrimack is seen moving steadily out to sea.

The Merrimack, when near the end of its long course, ex-

Short House, Old Newbury

pands into a noble basin enclosed within the sweep of picturesquely grouped and broken highlands. It is here every inch a river, broad, deep, clear, and sparkling. On one side are the hills of Amesbury and Salisbury, on the other side the city of Newburyport rises from the curved shore to the summit of the ridge, crowned with trees and spiked with steeples.

Down below the city and toward the sea all this changes. The high shores drop into fens, marshes, and downs. A long, low island thrusts itself half across the channel and blockades it. Beyond this again the sea breaks heavily on the low bar outside, and the river disappears in a broken line of foam.

John Quincy Adams once described Siberia as being celebrated for its malefactors and malachite. Some one, in an epigrammatic vein, has summed up Newburyport as being famous for piety and privateering; and the analogy seems established when one turns to the history of Newbury written by Whittier's old school-master, Joshua Coffin, and reads there that the privateersmen on putting to sea were accustomed to request the prayers of the churches for the success of the cruise — to which petition all those having a share in the voyage responded with a hearty amen.

Newburyport, then, is a city built upon a hill. One reads its history as he walks. Like Salem, it rose and flourished through its commerce, but when that failed, the business of the place had to be recast in a wholly different mould, and its merchants became spinners and weavers, instead of shipowners and shipbuilders.

The waterside street begins at a nest of idle shipyards, winds with the river along a line of rusty wharves, where colliers take the place of Indiamen, and ends with the antiquated suburb of Joppa — which at least retains some of the flavor of a seaport, it having

Tappan House at Newbury

a population that gets its living by fishing, piloting, or doing such odd jobs as watermen can pick up along shore. From here the sails of a vessel nearing the port could be seen gliding along over the sand-drifts of Plum Island or Salisbury Beach.

On High Street, on the cool brow of the ridge, are the stately homes of the wealthy citizens; here the old merchants, who amassed fortunes in West India rum and sugar in little stuffy count-ing-rooms on the wharves below, lived like princes in the great roomy mansions whose windows overlooked all the town, the silvery course of the river, and the surrounding country for miles up and down. Although they became sadly out of date, and of such size as to suggest that a blow of the hospitable knocker would fill them with echoes, there was an air of gentility and of good living about all these houses which makes us feel regret for the generation whose open-handed hospitality has passed into a tradition.

Usually there was an observatory on the roof, from which the owner could sweep the offing with his glass of a morning, and could run over in his mind the chance of a voyage long before his vessel had wallowed over the bar outside. He might then descend, take his cocked hat and cane from the hall-table, order dinner, with an extra cover for his captain, pull out his shirt-frill, and go down to his counting-house without a wrinkle on his brow or a crease in his silk stockings; everybody would know that his ship had come in. Sound in head and stomach, bluff of speech, yet with a certain homely dignity always distinguishing his class, the merchant of the olden time, undoubted autocrat to his immediate circle of depend-ants, was a man whose like we shall not look upon again. He left no successors.

During the two wars with England, a swarm of privateers, as well as some of the most famous vessels of the old, the invincible, navy, were launched here. In 1812 the port suffered as long and rigorous a blockade from the enemy's cruisers, as before it had been nearly paralyzed by Jefferson's embargo. Then the merchant had ruin staring him in the face whenever he levelled his glass at

Swett-Ilsley House, Old Newbury. *Right*, Dalton House at Newbury-port

the two and three deckers exchanging signals in the offing, or when he paced up and down his grass-grown wharves, where his idle ships rusted; but if he did sometimes shut his glass with an angry jerk, or stamp his foot to say, between an oath and a groan, "Our masts take root, bud forth too, and beare akornes!" he was never found wanting in patriotism, nor did he show a craven spirit in the face of his reverses, so that the record of the Tracys, the Daltons, the Browns, is one of which their descendants are justly proud. Still, it was not thought to be a sinful thing in those days for the clergy to pray that a change of rulers might remove the embargo, or that a stiff gale of wind would raise the blockade.

For the 19th century visitor there were two things in Newburyport which he asked to see. One was the tomb of George Whitefield, and the other the mansion of Lord Timothy Dexter.

Two objects more diverse by their associations, two lives more opposite in their aspirations, it would be difficult to conceive of, yet here the memories of the two men jostle each other.

The number of pilgrims who visited the tomb of Whitefield was formerly very large. The great itinerant preacher was buried in a vault that is entered by a door underneath the pulpit of the Old South Presbyterian meeting-house, in Federal Street. Its slender and modest spire, with its brazen weathercock, rose above a neighborhood no longer fashionable, perhaps, but quite in keeping with its own severe simplicity. The house has the date 1756 over the entrance-door, and is built of wood. At the left of the pulpit is a marble cenotaph erected to the memory of Whitefield, one face of which bears a long, eulogistic inscription. Descending into the crypt, whose sepulchral darkness a lamp dimly lights, we are alone with its silent inmates. A dark object shapes itself into a bier. We approach it. The coffin-lid is thrown open, so as to expose what is left of its tenant — the fleshless skull and bones of George Whitefield. It is not forbidden to shudder. Who, indeed, that looks can believe that "there, Whitefield, pealed thy voice"?

Owing, doubtless to the fact that many come to gratify an idle curiosity, the trustees closed the tomb; "for a spell" as the old sexton remarked, with too evident vexation for the loss of his fees for showing it to visitors. It is a curious instance of vandalism that one of the arm-bones should have been surreptitiously taken from the coffin, and after having twice crossed the ocean, have found its way back to its original resting-place. The story goes that an ardent admirer of the eloquent preacher, who wished to obtain some relic of him, gave a commission to a friend for the purpose, and this friend, it is supposed, procured the limb through the connivance of the sexton's son. The act of desecration being discovered, aroused so much indignation that the possessor thought it best to relinquish his prize; he accordingly intrusted it to a shipmaster, with the injunction to see it safely placed in the vault with his own eyes, which direction was strictly carried out. "And I," finished the sexton, "have been down in the tomb with the captain who brought that ar' bone back." But this all happened many years ago.

This neighborhood is further interesting as being the birth-place of William Lloyd Garrison, whose dwelling was the first on the left in School Street, while the next was that in which White-field died of an attack of asthma. The extraordinary religious awakening that followed his preaching is one of the traditions common to all New-England seaboard towns, the houses where he stopped being always pointed out; so that everywhere Whitefield has a monument. A missionary who crossed the ocean fourteen times, an evangelist who preached more than 18,000 sermons, and whose audiences were so numerous that he was compelled to hold his meetings in the open air, was no ordinary man. To this expo-sure of himself his death is attributed. It caused a deep sensation; and so much had the public estimate of him changed, that there was even a contention for the honor of possessing his remains, which now lie in the place where he was stoned when he first at-tempted to preach in it. Such is the retribution that time brings. When this cowardly assault nearly struck the Bible from his hand, the man who always had an answer for everything, holding up the book, said with calm dignity but in a voice that went through his hearers like an electric shock: "I have a warrant from God to preach; his seal is in my hand, and I stand in the King's highway."

Lord Timothy Dexter of Newburyport

Timothy Dexter was not born great, neither did he have greatness thrust upon him; yet so effectively does he seem to have thrust his quasi-greatness upon Newburyport that even after the lapse of many years strangers still asked to be guided to the spot where the renowned Lord Timothy lived in most unrepublican state.

Timothy Dexter was not a native of Newburyport, but of Malden. Although bred to the tanner's trade, Timothy was far too shrewd to hide his talents in a vat. He saw easier avenues to wealth opening before him, and he bought and sold until he had accumulated a snug capital for future speculations.

Having put money in his purse, Timothy Dexter became ambitious, believing that a golden key would admit him within the circles of aristocracy. Then as now Newburyport was the seat of culture, refinement, and literature, and it was therefore to Newburyport that the titled tanner turned his eyes. He found two mansion houses available for his purpose and these he purchased. The first, on State Street, he soon sold at a profit, and then he removed to the estate on High Street, making it one of the historic mansions of Essex County.

He now began the work of renovation which transformed the sober mansion of his predecessor into a harlequinade in wood. By his directions the painters adorned the outside a brilliant white, trimmed with green. Minarets were built on the roof, in the center of which rose a lofty cupola surmounted by a gilded eagle with outspread wings. Standing upon the crown of the hill, the house could be seen for miles around, and soon became a landmark for mariners. But the great and unique display was made in the garden fronting this house.

There was working at his trade in the town a skilful ship-carver named Wilson, whom Dexter employed to carve from the solid wood some forty gigantic statues of the most celebrated men of the period. These images were about eight feet in height. With conscientious fidelity to fact and fitness, the carved clothing was painted to resemble that worn by the real personages, — blue coats, white shirts, buff breeches, and the rest, — altogether making a display no museum could equal. Over the main entrance to the house, on a beautiful arch, stood George Washington, with John Adams, bareheaded, at his right hand; for Dexter said that no one should stand covered on the right hand of his greatest hero. On the left was Thomas Jefferson, holding a scroll inscribed Constitution. Lord Timothy, it is said, in spite of the painter's objections, insisted upon spelling the name of the Sage of Monticello, Tomas instead of Thomas, finally threatening to shoot the artist if he persisted in his refusal to do what was required of him.

The man who planned and created this garden of statues was as capricious as fame itself. If he raised a statue to some favorite to-day, he reserved the right to change his name tomorrow; and often a stroke of the painter's brush transformed statesmen into soldiers, or soldiers into civilians. General Morgan yesterday was Bonaparte to-day, to whom Dexter always paid the civility of touching his hat when he passed underneath the great Corsican's shadow. In the panels of the entablatures on which these images stood were the names of the characters represented. Among them were Rufus King, General Butler of South Carolina, General Henry Knox, John Jay, John Hancock, William Pitt, Louis XVI., King George, Lord Nelson, and the Indian Chief, Corn Planter. There was also one allegorical figure representing Maternal Affection, and another a Travelling Preacher, besides several enormous lions occupying pedestals. Dexter himself monopolized two statues. One of these stood near the door, holding in its hand a placard, which was inscribed, "I am first in the East, the first in the West, and the Greatest Philosopher in the known world." The cost of these images, with the columns on which they were placed, is said to have been $15,000. This was the only way, however, in which Lord Timothy was able to bring himself into association with greatness. Society refused him recognition with the same hard obduracy that his own wooden images did, his vulgarity and ignorance being too gross even for all his gold to gild; and so he lived only among sycophants and parasites, who cajoled and flattered him to his heart's content.

Having a house and grounds which he flattered himself would make his stuck-up neighbors split with envy, Dexter next resolved to set up an equipage fit for a lord; and one suiting his ideas of magnificence was accordingly procured. Some one having told him that the carriages of the nobility were always decorated with a coat of arms, one was composed on demand and painted on the panel.

In the matter of horses Dexter was extremely fastidious, as well as capricious. As soon as he grew tired of one color, he would sell those he had just bought at extravagant prices, and buy others. His costly carriage, drawn by beautiful cream-colored animals, became one of the sights of the day whenever the owner chose to take an airing; but to the luxury of the equipage the gaunt and mean face, half buried underneath an enormous cocked-hat, the spare figure sitting bolt upright, the hairless dog squatted beside it, offered a contrast strikingly ridiculous. In this coach Dexter once drove in state to the county prison at Ipswich, where he served a short sentence for firing his pistol at a countryman who stood staring at his museum of celebrities, and who did not move on when my Lord Timothy commanded him.

But this singular being did not consider his establishment as complete without the *entourage* of a nobleman in the days of chivalry. He would again revive the age of poets and troubadours. Perhaps the most unique idea of all was the engagement of a poet-laureate to write his praises and to embalm his memory in verse. There happened to be living in Newburyport one Jonathan Plummer, an eccentric pedler of fish, who had a flair for extempore rhyming which with the ignorant and illiterate passed for genius. A bargain was forthwith struck with him to serve in the capacity of poet-laureate, and as such he was presently installed in Dexter's household. A handsome new livery was ordered, consisting of a fine black broadcloth coat, with stars on the collar and fringe on the skirts, shoes with large silver buckles, a cocked-hat, and a gold-headed cane.

Dexter's unique speculation in warming-pans, told by himself, perhaps has done more to transmit his name to posterity than anything else. He relates that, having dreamed three nights running that warming-pans would do well in the West Indies, he collected "no more than 42,000," which were put on board nine vessels bound to different ports, and cleared him seventy-nine per cent. The story goes that one of Dexter's captains took off the covers of the pans and then sold them to the sugar-planters, who were anxious to obtain them for ladles.

Dexter's speculations in whalebone and Bibles were equally comical and absurd. Again he dreamed "that the good book was run down in this country so low as half price, and dull at that. I had," he says, "the ready cash by wholesale. I bought 21,000. I put them into twenty-one vessels for the West Indies, and sent as a text that all of them must have one Bible in each family, or they would go to —— ."

Besides putting faith in dreams, Dexter believed in fortune-telling as well as fortune-making, and made many attempts to pry into the future. A person who is said to have exerted great influence for good over this eccentric man was a negress named Lucy Lancaster, who is described as being possessed of unusual shrewdness

On the Common at Newburyport where Washington is commemorated. *Right*, eighteenth century houses on High Street, Newburyport

and information. Her father, called Caesar, was the son of an African king, and was brought to the country as a slave. When the yellow fever raged in Newburyport in 1796, Lucy Lancaster proved herself indeed of royal blood. Strong and fearless, she devoted herself day and night to the sick; Dexter, having need of her services, she became a firm friend and counsellor to the family. Her estimate of Dexter was much higher than the common one, and she gave him credit for more honesty of purpose than most people did. He needed some one like her to advise him, and she frequently turned his attention from mischievous pursuits by suggesting alterations and improvements in his house and grounds. This woman survived Dexter nearly forty years.

One of the oddest of Dexter's freaks was his mock funeral, which he arranged with all the solemnity requisite for a real interment. In his garden he had caused to be built a spacious tomb, while in his house he had long kept a costly coffin of mahogany, richly adorned. With a curiosity perhaps unprecedented in the history of vain man, he wished to see the effect his funeral would produce. Invitations were issued, mourning apparel was prepared for his family, some one was found to officiate as minister, and the procession was duly formed, and marched to the vault in the garden. While this farce was performing, Dexter was looking from an upper window, and before the company had dispersed, he was found beating his wife for not shedding tears at his pretended demise.

One report says that Dexter, becoming dissatisfied with his wife, made a bargain with her to leave him, giving her $1,000, or perhaps $2,000 in exchange for his liberty. He then advertised for another wife, but there being no applicant, he was glad to hire his own wife to come back by the offer of a sum equal to that he had originally given her to go away.

On October 26, 1806, Lord Dexter died in his mansion on High Street. His funeral was an occasion which it would have pleased him to witness, but as the town officers would not, for sanitary reasons, allow his remains to be deposited in his garden tomb, he was laid away among his fellow townsmen in the public burying-ground near the frog pond.

Not long after his death a gale blew down many of the images, and the place grew dilapidated. About the year 1846, while it was being used as a factory boarding-house, the estate was purchased by a Newburyport man who possessed wealth and taste, and he proceeded to obliterate as far as possible all traces of his predecessor's follies. The three presidents over the door were thrown down and demolished, the grounds were newly laid out and soon nothing except the eagle on the summit of the cupola remained to show Dexter's bizarre achievements in ornamentation, or to point a moral upon his extravagances as a philosopher.

Onion Field near Newbury

MOLL PITCHER,
THE FORTUNE-TELLER OF LYNN

IN PASSING from the boundaries of Saugus into those of Lynn, a word or two acquaints us with the origin of both places. Thomas Dudley, Deputy Governor of "the Massachusetts," writing in 1630 to the Lady Bryget, Countesse of Lincoln, says of the Colonists who, like himself, emigrated in that year from England: "We began to consult of the place of our sitting down, for Salem, where we landed, pleased us not." Various causes having led to their dispersion along the coast from Cape Ann to Nantasket. One of the scattered bands settled "upon the river of Saugus," as he writes; another founded Boston. The Indian name Saugus, which still belongs to the river and to a fragment of the ancient territory, was superseded in 1637 by that of Lynn, or the King's Lynn, from Lynn Regis, on the River Ouse, in England. Lynn is therefore one of the oldest towns in Massachusetts. It is beautifully situated on the shore of Massachusetts Bay, ten miles north of Boston and five south of Salem. Swampscott is a rib taken from her side; so is Nahant, and so is Lynnfield; yet, like the fabled monster, she seems to grow the faster from successive mutilations.

One of the earliest settlers, Francis Ingalls, established the first tannery in the Colony, and may be considered originator of that branch of industry that has made Lynn both rich and famous. When shoemaking was a trade, I suppose nearly every man in Lynn was a shoemaker, but now (1888) when no one person makes a whole boot or a whole shoe, the trade, as a trade, has degenerated. The poet Whittier once followed this humble calling, and the philanthropist William Lloyd Garrison once worked at the bench here in Lynn.

But Lynn is likely to be celebrated as the residence of the most successful fortune-teller of her generation. She lived at the foot of a cliff of dull red porphyry called High Rock. During the fifty years that she pursued her trade of fortune-telling in what was then a little frequented quarter of the town, she was consulted not only by the poor and ignorant, but also by the rich and intelligent class. Love affairs, legacies, the discovery of crime, lotteries, commercial ventures and the more common contingencies of fortune formed the staple of her predictions, but her most valued clients came from the opulent seaports that are within sight of High Rock. The common sailor and the master, the cabin-boy and the owner, equally resorted to her humble house to learn the luck of a voyage. It is said that many a vessel was deserted on the eve of sailing, in consequence of Moll's unlucky vaticination. She was also much besought by treasure-seekers — a rather numerous class in her day, whose united digging along the coast of New England, if usefully directed, would have reclaimed for cultivation no inconsiderable area of virgin soil. "Fools!" she would say; "if I knew where money was buried, do you think I would part with the secret?"

Moll Pitcher died in 1813, at the age of seventy-five. She was originally of Marblehead, and is said to have inherited the gift of prophecy from her grandfather, John Dimond, who was himself a wizard of no mean reputation in that place. In proof of this it is said that he was in the habit of going to the old burying-ground on the hill whenever a violent gale at sea arose. He would direct vessels then at sea how to weather the roughest gale — pacing up and down among the gravestones, and in a voice distinctly heard above the howling of the tempest, shout his orders to the helmsman or the crew, as if he were actually on the quarter-deck. Very few doubted his ability to bring a vessel safely into port. Mary Dimond's father sailed out of Marblehead as master of a small vessel. She married Robert Pitcher, a shoemaker, in 1760. Her life seems to mark the line that divides old and new superstition, rather than any decline of that inextinguishable craving to pry into futurity which has distinguished the human race in all ages.

Bass Rocks at Gloucester

PIRATES OFF
THE NEW ENGLAND COAST

D URING the first quarter of the 18th century the seacoasts swarmed with freebooters, whose depredations upon our commerce are the themes of some of the most startling episodes in the history of piracy. Blackbeard, Low and Phillips stand preeminent in this list.

In the course of his last piratical cruise, from Jamaica to Newfoundland, Phillips fell in with and captured the sloop *Dolphin*, Andrew Harraden, master, belonging to Cape Ann. The *Dolphin* being a better vessel than his own, the pirate transferred his black flag to her, sending the crew away in another of his prizes. Captain Harraden was, however, detained a prisoner on board his own vessel. Two of the pirate crew, John Fillmore, of Ipswich, and Edward Cheesman, were men whom Phillips had taken out of ships he had plundered and pressed into his service, thus making them pirates against their will. Being found useful, Cheesman has been given the post of ship's carpenter shortly before the *Dolphin* was captured. Both he and Fillmore, however, were brave young fellows, and both had fully determined to take

121

the first opportunity of escaping from Phillips' clutches; but the watchfulness of the older pirates was such that they could get no opportunity of talking to each other except when pretending to be asleep, or playing at cards together. But by stealth they came to an understanding.

To Captain Harraden these two men broached their purpose, and finding him willing to strike a blow for the recovery of his vessel and his liberty, they with four confederates, already pledged to stand by them, fixed the day and the hour for making the attempt.

When the appointed hour of noon arrived, Cheesman, the leader, with Fillmore and Harraden, were on deck, as also were Nut, the master of the *Dolphin*, a fellow of great strength and courage, the boatswain, and some others of the pirate crew. Of all on board, Nut and the boatswain were the two whom the conspirators most feared to encounter. Cheesman, however, promised to take care of the master if the others would attend to the boatswain. No firearms were to be used. The attack was to be made and possession of the deck gained before the alarm could spread below.

Cheesman, having left his working tools on deck, as if he were going to use them about the vessel, walked aft to begin with the master; but seeing some signs of timidity in Harraden, he came back, gave him and his mates a dram of brandy each, drinking to the boatswain and the master the toast, "To our next merry-meeting." He then took a turn up and down the deck with Nut, in order to occupy the pirate's attention, while Fillmore, as if in sport, picked up the carpenter's axe from where it was lying and began to twirl it around on the point.

This was the signal agreed upon. Cheesman instantly grappled with the master, and after a brief struggle pitched him over the side into the sea. Fillmore, rushing upon the boatswain, with one blow of the axe laid him dead upon the deck. The noise of the scuffle brought the pirate chief on deck, but Cheesman quickly

The unending action of the Atlantic on the land

disabled him with a blow from the carpenter's mallet, which fractured his jawbone. Having armed himself with an adze, Harraden
then sprang upon Phillips with his uplifted weapon, but the gun-
ner of the pirate interposing between them, Cheesman tripped up
his heels, throwing him into the arms of a confederate, who flung
him overboard, after the master. Harraden then finished with
Phillips.

The conspirators then jumped into the hold and fell upon
the quartermaster, who was the only officer remaining alive, when
a young lad on board pleaded so earnestly for the quartermaster's
life that he was spared. The rest of the pirate crew was securely
put in irons and the vessel steered directly for Boston, where she
arrived on the 3d of May, 1724, to the great joy of the people of
the province. Two of the pirates, Archer, the quartermaster, and
William White, were tried, convicted, and executed. Fillmore,
Cheesman, and their confederates were honorably acquitted. John
Fillmore, the pirate in spite of himself, was the great-grandfather
of the thirteenth President of the United States.

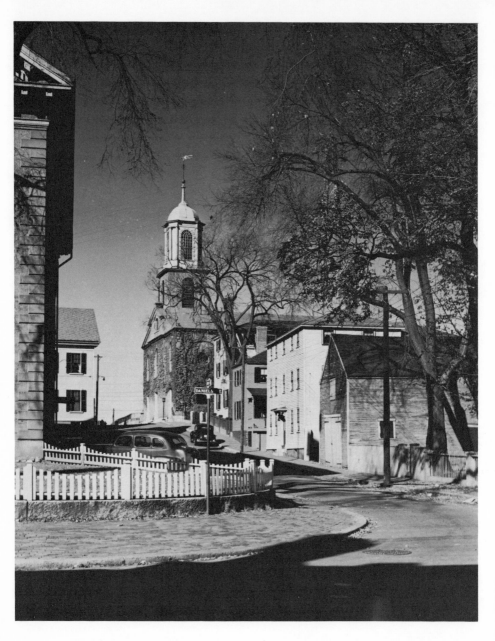

Chapel Street, Portsmouth, leading to the Piscataqua River Harbor

LEGENDS OF OLD PORTSMOUTH

THE EARLY voyagers soon discovered the Piscataqua River and quickly perceived its advantages as a harbor. There was Agamenticus for a landmark, and there was the swift-flowing tide, which the natives told them was never frozen. There were spacious basins, deep and sheltered, in which a navy might ride securely, and there were also high and gently sloping banks, over which the swaying pines looked down upon their own dark shadows in the eddying stream below. The river was found to conduct into a fertile and heavily-timbered region, of which it was the natural outlet. The shores were seen to afford admirable sites for the settlement that one and the other were destined to support.

This was accordingly begun in 1623, under the direction and authority of Gorges and Mason, in whom the successful experiment of the Plymouth Pilgrims had inspired new hopes of turning their royal grants to account.

The promoters of the settlement were churchmen, who had little sympathy with the Puritan ideas, and none at all with its scheme of government; and as some of those who had found these ideas too hard for their stomachs had removed into New Hampshire, a prejudice grew up between the two communities, which afford an example of two diverse systems growing up side by side. Wheelwright and his friends were of the latter class. Time, mutual interest, and the rapid ascendency obtained by the sister colony, with other considerations, finally closed the breach.

The system of Gorges and Mason, to establish a colony of tenants having leaseholds subject only to quit-rents, which they should govern by their agents, worked only evil to themselves. It was an attempt to graft the landed system of Old upon New England by the side of the freehold plan of the thrifty and sagacious Massachusetts patentees, and it was a disastrous failure. Finding that they were growing poor, while the Puritan freeholders were growing rich, the people threw off their yoke and sought a union with Massachusetts.

Still, the old leaven of prejudice survived in the descendants of the original inhabitants, who loved royalty and its forms, ad-

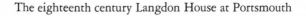

The eighteenth century Langdon House at Portsmouth

The Wentworth-Gardner House (1760) on the Piscataqua at Portsmouth. *Right*, the Langley-Boardman House in Portsmouth testifies
to prosperous times

hered to the mother church and its traditions, and felt no sympathy
for the austere manners, the rigid economy, or the quasi-ecclesi-
astical government of their more powerful neighbors. These people
gave tone to the principal settlement, and since there was no aristocracy of blood, one of wealth rose and flourished in its stead.

As the capital, the chief town, and the only seaport of the
province, Portsmouth long enjoyed a peculiar distinction. It remained the political center until the seat of government was transferred to the interior of the state. Inevitable changes turned
commerce into other channels. Its commercial importance waned,
progress was arrested, and the place came to a standstill, and for
several decades it was more remarkable for what it had been than
for what it was. Portsmouth had the stamp of an old coin. It had
the true weight and ring, but the date and the legend were old.

The best houses were still the oldest, and those of the Wentworths, Langdons, and Sherburnes, rivaled the traditional splendors of the Colonial mansions of the Puritan capital in spaciousness, richness of decoration, and that rare combination of simplicity and elegance that lifted the Colonial magnate above the heads of his own generation, and has made his housekeeping the admiration of ours. It is among these old houses that we must look for our legendary lore.

The West of England seaports are known to have furnished a great proportion of the original settlers in New England, and certainly no class were more susceptible to the influence of superstition than these sea-faring or sea-subsisting people. Upon the folklore of home was now grafted that of the Indian; over this again hovered the mystery of an unexplored country, in itself a keen spur to the appetite that grows with what it feeds upon. The region round about Portsmouth, Newcastle, Kittery, York, and the Isles of Shoals, is therefore prolific in legends of a homely and primitive kind; one of which is that of the stone-throwing devil.

Under the title of *Lithobolia*, the story of the stone-throwing devil was printed in London in 1698. It purports to be the narrative of an eye-witness, and is signed R. C. This tract, consisting of a few leaves only, is now extremely rare, but a synopsis of its contents was published in the *Wonderful Providences* of Increase Mather.

George Walton was an inhabitant of Portsmouth in 1682. He had incurred the bitter enmity of an old woman of the neighborhood by taking from her a strip of land to which she laid claim, and as she was believed to be a witch she was suspected of being at the bottom of the mischief that subsequently drove Walton's family to the brink of despair. She had told Walton that he should never peacefully enjoy the land he had wrested from her.

One Sabbath night in June a shower of stones rattled against the sides and roof of Walton's house. It came as unexpectedly as a summer hailstorm. When it had ceased, the startled inmates, who were in bed, hurried on their clothes and sallied out to see if they could discover the perpetrators of this outrage. They found the gate taken off the hinges and carried to a distance from the house, but could neither see nor hear anything of the stone-throwers.

While thus engaged, a second volley of stones whistled about their heads, which drove them back to the shelter of the house. They first went into the porch, but they were quickly pelted out of this into an inner chamber, where, having bolted and barred all the doors, they awaited the next demonstration of their assailants. Several had been struck and hurt, and all were in consternation. But the stone battery opened again presently, filling the room itself with flying missiles, which crashed through the casements, scattering the glass in every direction, came down the chimney, bounding and rebounding along the floor like spent cannonballs, while the inmates looked on in helpless amazement at what threatened to demolish the house over their heads. This bombardment continued, with occasional intermission, for four hours.

While it was going on, Walton was walking the floor of his chamber in great disorder of mind, when a sledge-hammer cast with vindictive force thumped heavily along the floor overhead, and, narrowly missing him, fell at his feet, making a great dent in the oaken floor; at the same time the candles were swept off the table, leaving him in total darkness.

All this might have been the work of evil-minded persons, but certain things convinced the family that the stones were hurled by demon hands. Some of the stones that were picked up were found to be hot, as if they had just been taken out of the fire. Notwithstanding that several of them were marked, counted, and laid upon a table, these same stones would afterward be found flying around the room. Upon examination, the leaden cross-bars of the casements were found to be bent outwardly, and not inwardly, showing conclusively that the stones came from within, and not from without. Finally, some of the maidens of the household were frightened upon seeing a hand or the apparition of a hand, thrust out of a window — there being, to their certain knowledge, no one in the room where it came from.

After Walton had returned to bed a heavy stone came crash-
ing through his chamber-door. He got up, secured the unwelcome
intruder, and locked it in his own chamber; but it was taken out
by invisible hands, and carried with a great noise into the next
room. This was followed by a brickbat. The spit flew up the chimney, and came down again, without any visible agency. This carni-
val continued from day to day with an occasional respite. Wher-
ever the master of the house showed himself, in the barn, the
field, or elsewhere, by day or by night, he was sure to receive a
volley. No one who witnessed them doubted for a moment that all
these acts proceeded from the malevolence of the suspected witch,
and an attempt was accordingly made to brew a powerful witch-
broth in the house, to exorcise her. But for some reason or other
its charm failed to work, and so the spell remained hanging over
the afflicted family.

Walton had a guest staying with him, who became the faithful recorder of what happened while the storm of stones rained
down upon the doomed dwelling. In order to soothe his mind, he
took up a musical instrument and began to play, when "a good big
stone" rolled in to join in the dance, while the player looked on in
amazement. Among other tricks performed by the mischievous
demon who had taken up its unwelcome residence among the
family, was that of taking a cheese from the press and crumbling
it over the floor; then the iron used in the press was found driven
into the wall, and a kettle hung upon it. Several cocks of hay that
had been mowed near the house were adroitly hung upon trees near
by; while the mischievous goblin, twisting bunches of hay into
wisps, stuck them up all about the house kitchen.

The relater of all these unaccountable doings admits that
certain sceptical persons persisted in believing that any or all of
them might have been the work of human beings, but as every
one credits what he wishes to credit, so this ancient writer appears
to mention the fact only with the view of exposing its absurdity.
Our own purpose is, not to decide between two opinions, but to

declare that people in general considered George Walton to be a victim of supernatural visitation, or, in other words, bewitched; and to show that the temper of his day was such, that any occurrence out of the common was sure to be considered either as emanating from heaven or from the bottomless pit. There were no such things as accidents; everything had some design.

The Royal Governor and His Lady

Governor Benning Wentworth of New Hampshire, a man of family, the owner of large estates, and endowed with a sufficiently exalted idea of his own importance, had matrimonial idiosyncrasies wholly at odds with the traditions of his class. He lived in his mansion at Little Harbor, where he received visits of ceremony, punctually drank the King's health, and presided over the sittings of his Majesty's Council for the province. All this, it may be assumed, added a good deal to his sense of personal dignity, and not a little to his vanity, besides exerting a certain influence upon provincial politics, by establishing a coterie, with its headquarters under his own roof. The old fellow liked display. He had his personal guard, he had his stud, and it was his ambition to have the best wine-cellar in the province. His house contained half a hundred apartments, all of which were probably in use when the Honorable Council met, at the Governor's bidding, to make a levy of troops for Louisburg, or to act on other matters of public concern. Business being over, the company repaired to the billiard-room or the card-rooms, to the stables or to the river, for relaxation — the oldsters to kill time, the youngsters to kill the ladies.

But this brave establishment lacked one thing to render it complete, — a mistress. The Governor had been left widowed and childless in his old age. He determined to marry again.

The world, had it been consulted in the matter, might have imposed upon him a bride of mature years and experience; above all, one taken from his own rank. But the Governor was not yet too old to be insensible to the charms of youth and beauty, and he proceeded to propose marriage to a young woman of Portsmouth, who possessed all the personal graces requisite in his eyes to make her Lady Wentworth. The lady, however, saw nothing but a gouty old man. She, having moreover formed another attachment, rejected the Governor, for whom she cared not a button, in favor of a young mechanic whom she dearly loved. This double wound to his love and vanity the old Governor determined to avenge, and he caused the bridegroom to be kidnapped by a press-gang and carried off to sea.

The Governor's second matrimonial venture was more fortunate. This time his eyes fell upon Martha Hilton, a saucy, red-lipped gypsy of the town, who is first introduced to us while carrying a pail of water — probably fresh-drawn from the town pump. Her feet are bare, her dress scarcely covers her decently, yet she belongs to one of the oldest families in the province. But she is charming, even in these mean habiliments.

The sight of the girl in this plight so incenses the sharp-tongued landlady of the Earl of Halifax inn, that she exclaims from her doorway, "You Pat! How dare you go looking so? You ought to be ashamed to be seen in the street!"

A house that kept growing — The Benning-Wentworth Mansion in Portsmouth, New Hampshire

Fireplace, doorway and, *below,*
A Colonial bedroom in the Benning-Wentworth Mansion, Portsmouth

The warm blood comes into the maiden's cheeks at this sharp reproof. She gives her head, and haughtily says: "No matter how I look, I shall ride in my chariot yet, ma'am!" and passes on, leaving Mistress Stavers nailed to her doorstep at such unheard-of presumption in a half-dressed slip of a girl.

Martha Hilton next makes her appearance in the kitchen of the Governor's mansion at Little Harbor. But she is not to stay here. One day the Governor gives a splendid banquet. The company is assembled, and among the red coats of the quality is the black one of the Reverend Arthur Brown, rector of the Episcopal church. The dinner is served; the wine circulates freely round the board, and the guests, having dined well, have reached the moment of supreme content, when the Governor whispers something to a servant, who goes out. Presently Martha Hilton, blushing like fire, walks into the room and takes her stand in front of the fireplace. She is now richly dressed, and would hardly be recognized as the girl seen in the street not long ago. Conversation ceases; all the guests look up to admire the beautiful woman.

The Governor rises from his chair, goes over to where Martha is struggling to maintain her self-possession, and then, addressing himself to the clergyman, says: "Mr. Brown, I wish you to marry me."

"To whom?" asks the bewildered rector.

"To this lady," replies the Governor, taking Martha's hand in his.

As the dumfounded rector remains speechless, the irascible old Governor becomes imperative.

"Sir," he says, "as the Governor of his Majesty's province of New Hampshire, I command you to marry me."

Thereupon the rector performed the ceremony; the maiden of twenty became the bride of the gouty old man of sixty, and thus her saucy answer came true. The incident provided Henry Wadsworth Longfellow with a theme for a poem.

THE OLD LITERARY CIRCLES
OF NAHANT

ABOUT three miles from where we stand, rising abruptly from the sea, is a castellated gray rock crowned with a lighthouse. Egg Rock, as it is called, is not more than eighty feet from sea to summit, but its isolated and lonely position, its bold outlines cut clean and sharp on the blue background, make it seem higher. This rocky islet, the former eyrie of wild sea-birds, is by far the most picturesque object of this picturesque shore. It is almost always seen encircled with a belt of white surf, while in violent storms the raging seas assail it with such tremendous impetuosity as to give the idea of a fortress beleaguered by the combined powers of sea and air. At such times it cannot be approached with safety. Then the lighthouse keeper, whatever his wants may be, can hold no communication with the shore, but is a prisoner during the pleasure of the gale.

There is a good road over the Long Beach; but when the tide is nearly down, a broad esplanade of sand beckons us aside from the embankment over which that is now built. Here the heavy farm-carts that are gathering seaweed leave scarcely a print of their broad-tired wheels. Stamp upon it with the foot, and see how hard and firm it is; or smile at the lightning it emits under the impact — your childhood's wonder. We pass over half an acre of sand, moulded in the impress of little wavelets that have left their print like cunning chiselling or like masses of sandy hair in crimp. There behind a clump of rocks crouches a sportsman, who is patiently waiting for twilight to come, when the black ducks and coots fly over; those stooping figures among the rocks are not treasure-seekers, but clam-diggers.

Having crossed the Long Beach, we betake ourselves again to the road which winds around the shore of Little Nahant to a second beach, half a mile long. We again leave this behind, to climb the rocky ascent of the greater promontory, then finding ourselves in the long street of the village. Nahant is tempting to artist or antiquary, but especially so to the man of refined literary tastes, who knows no greater enjoyment than to visit the spots consecrated by genius. In Jonathan Johnson's house Longfellow partly wrote *Hiawatha*; and here, at Nahant, was also the birthplace of *The Bells of Lynn*, which the poet heard, "Borne on the evening wind across the crimson twilight."

Somewhat farther on we descend into an enticing nook, shaded by two aged and gigantic willows. Here, in the modest cottage of Mrs. Hannah Hood, surrounded by old Dutch folios, John Lothrop Motley began his *Rise and Fall of the Dutch Republic*. By ascending the rise of ground beyond the Hollow we may see the roof of the cottage where William H. Prescott, who died, like Petrarch, in his chair, worked at *Ferdinand and Isabella, The Conquest of Mexico*, and *Philip II*. On the point beyond us, assisted by his gifted wife, Louis Agassiz produced *Brazil*. Nathaniel Willis, George W. Curtis, Lydia H. Sigourney, and an admiring host of lesser celebrities who have felt its magnetic influence, celebrated Nahant in prose or verse. And the privilege of traversing her rocky shores, with Longfellow or Agassiz for a guide, was indeed something to be remembered by the scholars of the 19th century.

The Hollow seems the proper standpoint for a brief glance at the history of Nahant, down to the time when it became the retreat of culture, refinement, and wealth. Nahant (the twins) is a musical Indian name that trips lightly from the tongue. On the map it looks like the wyvern of heraldry, hanging to the coast by its tail. It was sold by Poquanum, a sagamore, in 1630, to the Lynn settlers, who used it in common as a pasture. Being to all intents an island, or rather two islands, at high tide, it was named the Fullerton Isles, in 1614, by Captain John Smith. It had been granted in 1622 to Captain Robert Gorges; but his title seems to have lapsed, and not to have been successfully revived. Under the rule of Andros, his favorite, Randolph, tried to steal it. The price originally paid for Nahant was a suit of clothes. In the earlier accounts, the two peninsulas appear to have been well wooded, but, in common with all the coastal islands, the natural forest disappeared and Nahant remained almost treeless until Thomas H. Perkins, a wealthy Boston merchant, planted several thousand shade-trees. His efforts to make Nahant a desirable summer residence were effectively seconded by Frederick Tudor, the ice-king, by Cornelius Coolidge, and other men of wealth and taste. Its name and fame began to resound abroad. A hotel was built in 1819, and a steamboat began to ply in the summer months between Boston and the peninsulas. In 1853 Nahant threw off its allegiance to Lynn, and became a separate town. Its earlier frequenters were, with few exceptions, wealthy Boston or Salem families.

The admirably kept roads lead where the most engaging sea-views are to be had. You lean over a railing and look down eighty feet to the bottom of a cove, where the sea ripples without breaking, and the clean, smooth pebbles chase back the refluent wave with noisy chatter. The tawny rocks wear coats of grass-green velvet; the perfume of sweet-fern and of eglantine is in the air. The cliffs of the eastern headland are very fine. It takes one's breath away to witness the rush and roar of the eternal surges among their iron ribs; yet the effect seems little more than would be produced by a hungry lion licking the bars of his cage. In a few instances, such as Castle Rock and the Devil's Pulpit, the rocks arise in regular castellated masses; but in general they are as much the expression of chaos of form as we might expect to see in the broken arches and colonnades of the earth's foundations. Being pitched about in fantastic yet awful confusion, they present curious accidental formations, or are split from summit to foundation-stone in chasms deep and gloomy, where the seething waters hiss and boil, much as they might have done when these colossal masses were first cooling. Here and there on the shores the sea has neatly hollowed out the natural curiosities locally known as the Natural Bridge, Swallows' Cave, Irene's Grotto, and the Spouting Horn.

The sea-view from the portico of the chapel, situated on the highest point of the headland, is one of the rarest on the coast, embracing many miles of the mainland from Lynn to the extreme point of Cape Ann, of the South Shore from Scituate to Boston Light, a slender, shapely, and minaret-like tower set on a half-submerged ledge at the entrance to Boston Harbor. On a clear day the dusky gray pillar of Minot's Light, and by night its ruddy flash, on the south coast, are visible.

Longfellow's summer residence was on the southern shore, which is less precipitous, but more sheltered from the bleak winds, than the northern shores are. Prescott also lived on the southern shore, on a rocky point not far from the Swallows' Cave, named by him Fitful Head. Agassiz' cottage, on the contrary, was on the north shore. It was a modest building, all upon the ground, and was probably better suited to the great scientist's simple tastes than the handsome villas of his eminent literary neighbors. Possibly it may have reminded him of his native land, "the beautiful Pays du Vaud."

CAPE COD TOWNS

Cape Cod is the bared and bended arm of Massachusetts: the shoulder is at Buzzard's Bay; the elbow, or crazy-bone, at Cape Mallebarre; the wrist at Truro, and the sandy fist at Provincetown — behind which the State stands on her guard, with her back to the Green Mountains, and her feet planted on the floor of the ocean, like an athlete protecting her Bay — boxing with northeast storms, and, ever and anon, heaving up her Atlantic adversary from the lap of earth — ready to thrust forward her other fist, which keeps guard the while upon her breast at Cape Ann.

HENRY D. THOREAU, 1855

THIS SANDY fist at Provincetown curls toward the wrist in such fashion as to form a semicircular harbor, famous as the New World haven which first gave shelter to the *Mayflower* and her sea-worn company. On the 21st of November, 1620, by our modern reckoning (November 11, Old Style), the Pilgrims after their

139

two bleak months of ocean, cast anchor here, rejoicing in the sight and smell of "oaks, pines, junipers, sassafras and other sweet wood." Here they signed their memorable compact, forming themselves into a "civil body politic," and covenanting with one another, as honest Englishmen, to "submit to such government and governors as we should by common consent agree to make and choose." Upon the adoption of this simple and significant constitution the Pilgrim Fathers, still on board the *Mayflower* in Provincetown harbor, proceeded to set in motion the machinery of their little republic, for after this, wrote Bradford, "they chose, or rather confirmed, Mr. John Carver (a man goodly and well-approved amongst them) their governor for one year." That same day a scouting party went ashore and brought back a fragrant boat-load of red cedar for firewood with a goodly report of the place.

These stout-hearted Pilgrims* were not the first Europeans to set foot on Cape Cod. Legends of the Vikings which drift about the low white dunes are as uncertain as the shifting sands themselves, and the French and Florentine navigators who sailed along the North American coast in the first half of the 16th century may have done no more than sight this sickle of land between sea and bay, but there are numerous records of English, French and Dutch visits, within the last twenty years before the coming of the *Mayflower*. It may be that no less a mariner than Sir Francis Drake was the first of the English to tread these shores, but that distinction is generally allowed to Captain Bartholomew Gosnold, who made harbor here in 1602 and was "so pestered with codfish" that he gave the Cape the name, which, said Cotton Mather, "it will never lose till the shoals of codfish be seen swimming upon the tops of its highest hills." Gosnold traded with the Indians for furs

---

* The Pilgrims of Plymouth never knew that they would become known to history by this term. Governor Bradford wrote "they knew they were pilgrims," meaning on a religious journey; many years later this term was applied to distinguish them from the other Massachusetts Bay settlements. All were Puritans, separatists from the Church of England.

The traditional wharves of Provincetown

and sassafras root and was followed the next year by Martin Pring, seeking a cargo of this latter commodity, then held precious in pharmacy. Within the next four years three French explorers touched at the Cape, and a French colony was projected, but came to nothing. The visit of Henry Hudson, too, left no trace. In 1614 that rover of land and sea, Captain John Smith, took a look at Cape Cod, which impressed him only as a "headland of hills of sand, overgrown with scrubby pines, hurts (huckleberries) and such trash, but an excellent harbor for all weathers." After Smith's departure Hunt, his second in command, enticed a group of Nauset Indians on shipboard, carried them off, and sold them into slavery at Malaga, Spain, for twenty pounds a man. As a consequence of this crime, the Indians grew suspicious and revengeful, but nevertheless an irregular trade was maintained with them by passing vessels, until the pestilence that raged among the red men of the region from 1616 to 1619 interrupted communication.

Living quarters "at the rear" in Provincetown, have their own garden of blooms. *Below,* a Cape Cod Cottage in Provincetown, called the Town's Oldest House

The Pilgrims tarried in Provincetown harbor nearly a month. The compact had been signed, anchor dropped and the reconnaissance made on a Saturday. The Sunday following the first Pilgrim Sabbath in America was devoutedly kept with prayer and praise on board the *Mayflower,* but the next morning secular activities began. The men carried ashore the shallop which had been brought over in sections between decks and proceeded to put it together, while the women bundled up the soiled linen of the voyage and inaugurated the first New England Monday by a grand washing on the beach. On Wednesday Myles Standish mustered a little army of sixteen men, each armed with musket, sword and corselet, and led them gallantly up the wooded cape through boughs and bushes, nearly as far as the present town of Wellfleet. After two days the explorers returned with no worse injury than briar-scratched armor, bringing word of game and water springs, ploughed lands and burial mounds. William Bradford showed the noose of a deer trap, a "very pretty devise," that had caught him by the leg, and two of the sturdiest Pilgrims bore, slung on a staff across their shoulders, a kettle of corn. As the few natives whom the party had met fled from them, the corn had been taken on credit from a buried hoard. The following year the debt was scrupulously paid.

As soon as the shallop could be floated a larger expedition was sent by water along the south coast to seek a permanent settlement. Through wind and snow the Pilgrim fathers made their way up to Pamet River in Truro, the limit of the earlier journey. They did not succeed in agreeing upon a fit site for the colony, but they sought out the corn deposit and, breaking the frozen ground with their swords, secured ten bushels more of priceless seed for the springtime. On the return of the second expedition there was anxious discussion about the best course to pursue. Some were for settling on the Cape and living by the fisheries, pointing out the whales that sported every day about the anchored ship; but the Pilgrims were of agricultural habit and tradition and had reason enough just then to be weary of the sea. The situation was critical.

"The heart of winter and unseasonable weather," wrote Bradford, "was come upon us." The gradual slope of the beach made it always necessary to "wade a bow-shoot or two" in going ashore from the *Mayflower*, and these icy footbaths were largely responsible for the "vehement coughs" from which hardly one of the company was exempt.

Once more, on the 16th of December, the shallop started forth to find a home for the Pilgrims. Ten colonists, including Carver, Bradford and Standish, together with a few men of the ship's crew, volunteered for this service. It was so cold that the sleety spray glazed doublet and jerkin and "made them many times like coats of iron." The voyagers landed within the present limits of Eastham or Orleans, where, hard by the shore, a camp was roughly barricaded. One day passed safely in exploration, but at dawn of the second, when "after prayer," the English sat about their campfire at breakfast, "a great and strange cry" cut the mist, and on the instant Indian arrows, headed with deer-horn and eagle's claws whizzed about their heads. But little Captain Standish was not to be caught napping. "Having a snaphance ready," he fired in direction of the warwhoop. His comrades supported him manfully. Their friends in the shallop, themselves beset, shouted encouragement, and the savages, gliding back among the trees, melted into "the dark of the morning." After this taste of Cape Cod courtesy the Pilgrim fathers can hardly be blamed for taking to their shallop again and plunging on, in a stiff gale, through the toppling waves, until, with broken rudder and mast split in three, they reached a refuge in the harbor of Plymouth.

When the adventurers returned to the *Mayflower* with glad tidings that a resting-place was found at last, the historian of the party, William Bradford, had to learn that during his absence his wife had fallen from the vessel's side and perished in those December waters. Three more of the colonists died in that first haven, and there little Peregrine White began his earthly peregrinations. In view of all these occurrences — the signing of the compact in

How the *Mayflower* appeared in Plymouth Harbor;
the modern reproduction

Provincetown harbor, the first landing of the Pilgrims on the tip
of Cape Cod, the explorations, the first deaths and the first birth —
it would seem that Provincetown is fairly entitled to a share of
those historic honors which are lavished, none too freely but perhaps too exclusively, on Plymouth.

When the *Mayflower* sailed away, carrying William Bradford
and his tablets, the beautiful harbor and its circling shores were
left to a long period of obscurity. Fishers, traders and adventurers
of many nations came and went on their several errands, but these
visits left little trace. The Plymouth colonists, meanwhile, did not
forget their first landing point, but returned sometimes in the fishing season for cod, bass and mackerel, always claiming full rights
of ownership. This claim rested not only on their original brief
occupation, but on formal purchase from the Indians, in 1654 or
earlier, the payment being "2 brasse kettles, six coates, twelve

houes, 12 axes 12 knives and a box." In process of time, as the English settlers gradually pushed down the Cape, a few hovels and curing-sheds rose on the harbor shore, but the land was owned by Plymouth Colony until Massachusetts succeeded to the title. These Province lands were made a district in the charge of Truro in 1714, but in 1727 the Precinct of Cape Cod was set off from Truro and established under the name of Provincetown as a separate township. It was even then merely a fishing hamlet with a fluctuating population, which by 1750 had almost dwindled away. In Revolutionary times it had only a score of dwelling houses and its 200 inhabitants were defenseless before the British, whose men of war rode proudly in the harbor. One of these, the *Somerset*, while chased by the French fleet on the Back Side, as the Atlantic coast of the Cape was called, struck on Peaked Hill bars, and the waves, taking part with the rebels, flung the helpless hulk far up the beach. Stripped by "a plundering gang" from Provincetown and Truro, the frigate lay at the mercy of the sands, and they gradually hid her even from memory, but the strong gales and high tides of 1886 tore that burial sheet aside and brought the blackened timbers again to the light of day. The grim old ship, tormented by relic hunters, peered out over the sea, looking from masthead to masthead for the Union Jack and, disgusted with what she saw, dived only more under her sandy cover, where the beach grass now grows over her.

A relic on the sands at Provincetown

Up and down the sandy knolls behind the streets straggle populous graveyards, where one may read the fortunes of Province-town more impressively, if less precisely, than in the census reports. Where the goodly old Nathaniels and Shubaels and Abrahams and Jerushas rest, a certain decorum of green sodding and white head-stone is maintained, despite the irreligious riot of the winds. The Catholic burial-ground, too, is not uncared for in its Irish portion. Marble and granite monuments implore "Lord have mercy on the soul" of some Burke or Ryan or McCarty, but the Portuguese wanderers from the Cape Verde Islands and the Azores sleep the sleep of strangers, with no touch of tenderness or beauty about their dreary lodging. Only here or there a little Jacinto or Manuel or Antone has his short mound set about with fragments of clam-shell, as if in children's play. Some lots are enclosed, the black posts with rounded tops looking like monastic sentries, and a few headboards, with the painted name already rain-washed out of recognition, lean away from the wind. In the center of this gaunt graveyard, where the roaring Atlantic storms tear up even the coarse tufts of beach grass, a great gray cross of wood, set in a hill of sand, spread its weatherbeaten arms. The guardianship of the Church and the fellowship of the sea these Portuguese fisherfolk brought with them, and as yet America has given them nothing dearer. The Portuguese constituted a large proportion of the for-eign element in Barnstable County where, near the turn of the century, nearly nine-tenths of the people were of English descent. The protruding tip of Cape Cod easily catches such ocean drift as these western islanders, and they made their way as far up the Cape as Falmouth, where they watched their chance to buy old homesteads at low rates.

Journeying from Provincetown, "perched out on a crest of alluvial sand," up the wrist of the Cape, one sees the land a-making. At first the loose sand drifts like snow. Then the coarse marsh-grass begins to bind and hold it, low bushes mat their roots about it, and planted tracts of pitch-pine give the shifting waste a real stability. The Pilgrims found, they said, — but perhaps there was a Canaan dazzle in their eyes — their landing place well wooded and the soil "a spit's depth, excellent black earth." But now all sods and garden ground must be brought from a distance, and a mulberry or a sycamore, even the most stunted appletree that squats and cowers from the wind, is a proud possession. When President Dwight of Yale rode through Truro into Provincetown more than a century ago, he was amazed at the sterility and bleak desolation of the landscape, half hidden as it was by "the tempestuous tossing of the clouds of sand." He was told that the inhabitants were required by law to plant every April bunches of beach-grass to keep the sand from blowing. The national government, stirred by danger to the harbor, afterwards took the matter in hand. Massachusetts became aroused to the desolate condition of her Province lands and made a determined effort to redeem them by the planting of trees and by other restorative measures. These blowing sand dunes, have however a strange beauty of their own, and the color effects in autumn, given by the low and ragged brush, are of the warmest.

"It was like the richest rug imaginable," wrote Thoreau, "spread over an uneven surface; no damask nor velvet, nor Tyrian dye or stuffs, nor the work of any loom could ever match it. There was the incredibly bright red of the huckleberry, and the reddish brown of the bayberry, mingled with the bright and living green of small pitch-pines, and also the duller green of the shrub oaks, and the various golden and yellow and fawn-colored tints of the birch and maple and aspen — each making its own figure, and, in the midst, the few yellow sand-slides on the sides of the hills looked like the white floor seen through rents in the rug."

Truro, the Indian Pamet, was formally settled in 1709 by a few English purchasers from Eastham, having been occupied earlier only by irresponsible fishermen and traders. The new planters took hold with energy, waging war against blackbirds and crows, wolves and foxes, for the protection of their little wealth in corn and cattle, while none the less they dug clams, fished by line and net and watched from their lookouts for offshore whales. The Cape plumes itself not a little upon its early proficiency in whaling. In 1690 one Ichabod Paddock, whose name might so easily have been Haddock, went from Yarmouth to Nantucket "to instruct the people in the art of killing whales in boats from the shore." And when the sea monster, thus maltreated, withdrew from its New England haunts, the daring whalemen built ships and followed, cruising the Atlantic and Pacific, even the Arctic and Antarctic oceans. But the American Revolution put a check on all our maritime enterprises. The Truro fishermen, like the rest, laid by their harpoons and melted up their mackerel leads for bullets. From one village of twenty-three houses, twenty-eight men gave up their lives for liberty. In religion, too, Truro had the courage of her convictions, building the first Methodist meeting-house on the Cape, the second in New England. The cardinal temptation of Cape Cod is Sunday fishing, and Truro righteousness was never put more sharply to the pinch than in 1834, when a prodigious school of blackfish appeared off Great Hollow one autumnal Sab-

Leyden Street in Plymouth, trod by the Pilgrims in 1620

bath morning. A number of Truro fishermen, from the Grand Banks and elsewhere, were on their way home in boats from Provincetown when the shining shoulders of hundreds of the great fish were seen moving through the waves. With fortunes in full view, a goodly number of these men shifted into boats which rowed soberly for their destination, while the rest, with eager out-cry, rounded up the school and drove the frightened creatures, with shouts and blows from the oars, like sheep upon the beach. Church-members who took part in the wild chase were brought to trial, but a lurking sympathy in the hearts of their judges saved them from actual expulsion. This befell within the period of Truro's highest prosperity. From 1830 to 1855 the wharves were crowded with sloops and schooners, a shipyard was kept busy, and salt was made along the shore. But the "turtle-like sheds of the salt works," which Thoreau noted, long since have been broken up and sold for lumber.

Although the sand of Cape Cod is in some places 300 feet deep, there is believed to be a backbone of deluvian rock. There is a clay vein, too, which slants across the Cape and crops out at Truro in the so-called Clay Pounds, now crowned by Highland Light, shining 200 feet above the ocean. This hill of clay renders a sovereign service to that dangerous stretch of navigation. It must be borne in mind that Cape Cod runs out straight into the Atlantic for two-score miles, by the south measurement, and then, abruptly turning, juts up another forty to the north. The shifty sandbars of the Back Side have caught, twisted and broken the hulls of innu-merable craft. One gale of wind wrecked eighteen vessels between Race Point at the extremity of the Cape and Highland Light. The average width of our crooked peninsula is six miles, but at Truro it narrows to half that distance. Across this strip the storms whirl the flinty sand until the humblest cottage may boast of ground-glass window panes. The coast outline is ever changing and the restless dunes show the fantastic carvings of the wind. The houses cuddle down into the waxy hollows, with driftwood stacked at their

The Highland Light at North Truro. *Right*, shingles on clapboards on Wellfleet cottages, Cape Cod

back doors for fuel, and with worn-out fishnets stretched about the chicken yards. Here and there a pine tree abandons all attempt at keeping up appearances and lies flat before the blast. The ploughed fields are as white with sand as so many squares of beach, and the sea-tang is strong in the air.

Wellfleet, which drew off from Eastham in 1763, had once her hundred vessels at the Banks, her whaling schooners, built in her own yards from her own timber, and beds of oysters much prized by city palates. There was a time when forty or fifty sail were busy every season transporting Wellfleet shell fish to Boston. "As happy as a clam" might then have been the device of Wellfleet heraldry. But suddenly the oyster died, and although the beds have been planted anew, the ancient fame has not been fully regained. A town many of whose citizens spent more than half their lives on shipboard, was sure to suffer from our wars, peculiarly disastrous to seafaring pursuits. Early in the Revolution Wellfleet was constrained to petition for an abatement of her war tax, stating that her whale-fishery, by which nine-tenths of her people lived, was entirely shut off by British gunboats, and that the shell-fish industries, on which the remaining tenth depended, was equally at a standstill. In this distress, as again in the Civil War, Cape Cod sailors took to privateering and made a memorable record.

The place abounds in dim old stories, from the colonial legend of the minister's deformed child, done to death by a dose from its father's hand — that child whose misshapen little ghost still flits on moonlight nights about a certain rosebush — to the many-versioned tale of the buccaneer, seen prowling about that point on the Back Side where Sam Vellamy's pirate ship was cast away, and stooping to gather the coins flung up to him by the skeleton hands of his drowned shipmates. A volume would not suffice for the stories of these Cape Cod towns. Their very calendar is kept by storms, as the Magee storm of December, 1778, when the government brig *General Arnold,* commanded by Captain James Magee, went down, or the Mason and Slidell storm of 1862, when the southern emissaries were brought from Fort Warren to Provincetown, and there, amidst the protest of the elements, yielded up to the British steamer *Rinaldo;* or the pitiless October gale of 1841, when from Truro alone 47 men were swallowed by the sea.

The old shingled windmill at Eastham

The quiet little town of Eastham, originally Nawsett, settled in 1646, only seven years after the three pioneers, Barnstable, Sandwich and Yarmouth, at the turn of the century found a resource in asparagus, shipping a carload or two to Boston every morning in the season. After the encounter between the Pilgrims and Indians here in 1620, the place was not visited again until the following July, when Governor Bradford sent from Plymouth a boatload of ten men to recover that young scapegrace, John Billington. This boy, whose father, ten years after, was hanged by the colonists for murder, had come near blowing up the *Mayflower* in Provincetown harbor, by shooting off a fowling-piece in her cabin, close by an open keg of powder, and later must needs loose himself in the Plymouth woods. He had wandered into the territory of the Nausets, who, although the tribe which had suffered from Hunt's perfidy, restored the lad unharmed to the English. The Nausets further proved their friendliness by supplying the Pilgrims, in the starving time of 1622, with stores of corn and beans. But the following year, suspecting an Indian plot against the colonists, Myles Standish, that "little chimney soon on fire," appeared on the Cape in full panoply of war, executed certain of the alleged conspirators and so terrified the rest that many fled to the marshes and miserably perished.

Eastham has more of a land look than the lower towns. The soil is darker, small stones appear, and the trees, although still twisted to left and right as if to dodge a blow, are larger. The Indians had maize fields there and the site seemed so promising to the Pilgrims that talk sprang up in the early forties of transferring the Plymouth colony thither. As a compromise several of the old-comers obtained a grant of the Nauset land and established a branch settlement, soon incorporated as a township. Promptly arose their meeting house, twenty feet square, with portholes and a thatch. They secured a full congregation by absence penalties of ten shillings, a flogging or the stocks. One of these sturdy fathers in the faith, Deacon Donne, is said to have lived to the patriarchal age of 110, rounding life's circle so completely that at the end, as at the beginning, he was helplessly rocked in a cradle.

Thoreau was amused over a provision made by the town of Eastham in 1662 that "a part of every whale cast on shore be appropriated for the support of the ministry," and drew a fancy picture of the old parsons, sitting on the sandhills in the storms, anxiously watching for their salaries to be rolled ashore over the bars of the Back Side. One of these worthies, the Reverend Samuel Treat, whose oratory outroared the stormy surf, shares with Richard Bourne of Sandwich the memory of a true pastoral care for the Cape Indians. He was in return so well beloved that on his death his wild converts dug a long passage through the remarkably deep snowfall of the time and bore him on their shoulders down this white pathway to his grave.

Orleans, set off in 1797 from the southerly portion of Eastham, received the distinction of being the terminus of the French Atlantic cable from Brest, in keeping with the name Orleans, a unique instance of a foreign title among these old Cape towns. The early settlers put by the melodious Indian words, Succanessett, Mattacheeset and the rest and substituted the dear home names from Devon, Cornwall, Norfolk and Kent. The christening of Brewster, Bourne and Dennis honored severally the Pilgrim elder, the Sandwich friend of the Indians, and a Yarmouth pastor. As Wellfleet and Orleans have been cut on north and south out of the original Eastham, so were Harwich, Chatham, Dennis, Brewster, once "within the liberties of Yarmouth."

Yarmouth, Barnstable and Sandwich were recognized as townships in 1639. From the outset the difference in their locations imposed upon them different tasks. Yarmouth, the elbow town of the Cape, bore the brunt of wind and wave; Sandwich kept the border, notably in King Philip's War, when she guarded the faithful Cape Indians from temptation and received for safe harborage English refugees from the ravaged districts; Barnstable, the aristocratic sister of the group, made traditions, set examples

Cape Cod cottages at Yarmouthport

The Julia A. Wood House, 1790, in Falmouth. *Right*, where the seventeenth century pioneers ground their corn: Sandwich, Cape Cod

and produced the Otis family. With Old Yarmouth the Cape widens. On the Back Side pine grove after pine grove adds flavor to the salt air, and where the carpet of needles is trodden through gleam patches of white sand. The strange reappearance of the *Somerset* is out-miracled in Old Ship Harbor, where, in 1863, long after the significance of the name had been forgotten, the hull of the *Sparrow-Hawk* wrecked there in 1626, on her way from London to Virginia, rose again to view. This portion of the Cape is in excellent repute with pleasure-seekers, and the seaside cottage is ubiquitous, especially in beautiful Chatham, whose ever-changing shore takes the wildest raging of the surf. Harwich, which has gone through the regular stages of whaling, codding, mackerel-fishing and salt-making, cultivates in turn the summer boarder, but somewhat quizzically. Retired sea captains are not easily over-awed even by golf sticks, and retired sea captains in Harwich are as thick as cranberries.

The waters lap the grass-choked slopes of Barnstable, Cape Cod

Delivery by power boat at Chatham

In 1837 that little town of Dennis claimed no fewer than 150
skippers sailing from various American ports, and in 1850 it was
said that more sea captains went on foreign voyages from Brewster
than from any place in the United States. Often their wives sailed
with them and had thereafter something wider than village gossip
to bring to the quilting and the sewing circle. It was a great day
for the children in the village when a sea captain came home.
From door to door went his frank sailor gifts, jars of Chinese sweet-
meats, shimmering Indian stuffs, tamarinds, cocoanuts, parrots,
fans of gay feather, boxes of spicey wood, glowing corals and such
great whispering shells as Cape Cod never knew. It was a hospitable and merry time given to savory suppers, picnic clambakes and
all manner of neighborly good cheer. Even the common dread
made for a closer sympathy. Any woman, going softly to her neighbor to break the news of her husband lost in the Arctic ice, might
in some dark hour drop her head upon that neighbor's shoulder in
hearing of a son drowned off the banks or slain by South Sea
islanders.

The general history of Falmouth but repeats the story of her sister towns. The first settlers are believed to have come in boats from Barnstable in 1660. They encamped for the night among the flags of Consider Hatch's Pond, where a child was born and, in recognition of the rushes that sang his earliest lullaby, named Moses. The town was duly incorporated in 1686, next after Eastham, and has steadfastly stood for piety, wisdom and patriotism. She admitted the Quakers and if one of her deacons held a Negro slave, as colonial deacons often did, poor Cuffee was at least brought to the communion table. It is Truro that contains "Pomp's Lot," where the stolen African, with loaf of bread and jug of water at his feet for sustenance on his new journey, escaped slavery by hanging himself from a tree. As for learning, it was Sandwich Academy that the Cape towns held in awe, but our Falmouth men, like the rest, half sailor, half farmer and all theologian, had a genuine culture, born of keen-eyed voyaging and of lonely thought, that kept the air about them tingling with intelligence. When it comes to war stories, if Provincetown, from her end of the Cape, can tell of her boy in blue that went down with the *Cumberland* and her naval captain at Manila, Falmouth can recall that twice she was bombarded by the British and twice defended by the valor of her sons, and when the Civil War broke out, with the larger share of her able-bodied men at sea, she yet sent more than her quota of soldiers to the front.

PETER RUGG, THE ETERNAL WANDERER OF NEW ENGLAND

Fantasy frequently has dealt with the legend of the wandering man who never reaches his destination. He appears in various guises in European folklore and seems to have been revived in the tap rooms of New England inns. Here, as elsewhere, something strange and sinister is associated with his visits. The present version, credited to William Austin, takes the form of a letter describing incidents on the highways of more than a century ago.

AGREEABLY to my promise, I now relate to you all the particulars of the lost man and child that I have been able to collect. It is entirely owing to the humane interest you seemed to take in the report that I have pursued the inquiry to the following result.

You may remember that business called me to Boston in the summer of 1820. I sailed in the packet to Providence; and when I arrived there, I learned that every seat in the stage was engaged. I was thus obliged either to wait a few hours, or accept a seat with

159

the driver, who civilly offered me that accommodation. I soon found him intelligent and communicative. When we had travelled about ten miles, the horses suddenly threw their ears on their necks as flat as a hare's. Said the driver, "Have you a surtout with you?"

"No," said I; "why do you ask?"

"You will want one soon," said he. "Do you observe the ears of the horses? They see the storm-breeder, and we shall see him soon."

At this moment there was not a cloud visible in the firmament; soon after a small speck appeared in the road.

"There," said my companion, "comes the storm-breeder; he always leaves a Scotch mist behind him. By many a wet jacket do I remember him. I suppose the poor fellow suffers much himself — much more than is known to the world."

Presently a man with a child beside him, with a large black horse and a weather-beaten chair, once built for a chaise-body, passed in great haste, apparently at the rate of twelve miles an hour. He seemed to grasp the reins of his horse with firmness, and appeared to anticipate his speed. He seemed dejected, and looked anxiously at the passengers, particularly at the stage-driver and myself. In a moment after he passed us, the horses' ears were up, and bent themselves forward so that they nearly met.

"Who is that man?" said I; "he seems in great trouble."

"Nobody knows who he is; but his person and the child are familiar to me. I have met him more than a hundred times, and so often have been asked the way to Boston by that man, even when he was travelling directly from that town, that of late I have refused any communication with him; and that is the reason he gave me such a fixed look."

"But does he never stop anywhere?"

"I have never known him to stop anywhere longer than to inquire the way to Boston. He will tell you he cannot stay a moment, for he must reach Boston that night."

"Do you look," said he, "in the direction whence the man

came; that is the place to look. The storm never meets him, it follows him."

We presently approached another hill; and at the height the driver pointed out in an eastern direction a little black speck about as big as a hat. "There," said he, "is the seed storm; we may possibly reach Polley's before it reaches us, but the wanderer and his child will go to Providence through rain, thunder, and lightning."

In the meantime the distant thunder gave notice of a shower, and just as we reached Polley's tavern the rain poured down in torrents. It was soon over, the cloud passing in the direction of the turnpike toward Providence. In a few moments after, a respectable-looking man in a chaise stopped at the door. The man and child in the chair having excited some little sympathy among the passengers, the newcomer was asked if he had observed them. He said he had met them, that the man seemed bewildered and inquired the way to Boston; that he was driving at great speed, as though he expected to outstrip the tempest; the moment he had passed, a thunderclap broke directly over the man's head, and seemed to envelop both man and child, horse and carriage. "I stopped," said the traveler, "supposing the lightning had struck him; but the horse only seemed to increase his speed, and as well as I could judge, he travelled just as fast as the thundercloud."

This was all I could learn at that time; and the occurrence soon would have seemed like things that never happened, had I not, as I stood on the doorstep of Bennett's Hotel in Hartford, heard a man say, "There goes Peter Rugg and his child! He looks wet and weary, and farther from Boston than ever." I was satisfied it was the same man I had seen more than three years before, for whoever has seen Peter Rugg never after can be deceived as to his identity.

"Peter Rugg!" said I; "and who is Peter Rugg?"

"That," said the stranger, "is more than any one can tell exactly. He is a famous traveler, held in light esteem by all innholders, for he never stops to eat, drink, or sleep. I wonder why the Government does not employ him to carry the mail."

"But," said I, "does the man never stop anywhere? Does he never converse with any one? I saw the same man more than three years ago near Providence. Give me some account of this man."

"Sir," said the stranger, "those who know the most respecting that man say the least. I have heard it asserted that heaven sometimes sets a mark on a man either for judgment or trial. Under which Peter Rugg now labors, I cannot say; therefore I am rather inclined to pity than to judge."

"Has his appearance much altered in this time?"

"Yes, he looks as though he never ate, drank, or slept, and his child looks older than himself."

"And how does his horse look?"

"As for his horse, he looks fatter and gayer, and shows more animation and courage, than he did twenty years ago. The last time Rugg spoke to me he inquired how far it was to Boston. I told him just one hundred miles.

" 'Why,' said he, 'how can you deceive me so? It is cruel to mislead a traveler. I have lost my way; pray direct me the nearest way to Boston."

" 'But,' said I, 'you are now traveling from Boston. You must turn back.'

" 'Alas!' said he, 'it is all turn back! Boston shifts with the wind, and plays all around the compass. One man tells me it is to the east, another to the west, and the guide-posts, too, all point the wrong way.'

"Is Peter Rugg his real name?"

"I don't know, but presume he will not deny his name; you can ask him, for see, he has turned his horse, and is passing this way."

In a moment a dark-colored, high-spirited horse approached, and would have passed without stopping, but I had resolved to speak to Peter Rugg. Accordingly I stepped into the street, and as the horse approached, I made a feint of stopping him. The man immediately reined in his horse. "Sir," said I, "may I be so bold as to inquire if you are not Mr. Rugg? — for I think I have seen you before."

"My name is Peter Rugg," said he: "I have unfortunately lost my way. I am wet and weary, and will take it kindly of you to direct me to Boston."

"You live in Boston, do you? And in what street?"

"In Middle Street."

"When did you leave Boston?"

"I cannot tell precisely; it seems a considerable time."

"But how did you and your child become so wet? It has not rained here to-day."

"It has just rained a heavy shower up the river. But I shall not reach Boston to-night if I tarry. Would you advise me to take the old road, or the turnpike?"

Wayside Inn, South Sudbury, Massachusetts

"Why, the old road is one hundred and seventeen miles, and the turnpike is ninety-seven."

"How can you say so? You know it is but forty miles from Newburyport to Boston."

"But this is not Newburyport, this is Hartford."

"Do not deceive me, sir. Is not this town Newburyport, and the river that I have been following the Merrimac?"

"No, sir; this is Hartford, and the river the Connecticut."

I had now, as I thought, discovered a clew to the history of Peter Rugg, and determined, the next time my business called me to Boston, to make a further inquiry. Soon after, I was enabled to collect the following particulars from Mrs. Croft, an aged lady in Middle Street, who has resided in Boston for twenty years.

The last summer, a person, just at twilight, stopped at the door of the house formerly occupied by Mrs. Rugg. Mrs. Croft, on coming to the door, saw a stranger, with a child by his side, in an old weather-beaten carriage, with a black horse. The stranger asked for Mrs. Rugg, and was informed that Mrs. Rugg had died in a good old age more than twenty years before.

The stranger replied, "How can you deceive me so? Do ask Mrs. Rugg to step to the door."

"Sir, I assure you Mrs. Rugg has not lived here these nineteen years; no one lives here but myself, and my name is Betsey Croft."

"Madam! you cannot be serious. But you doubtless know my brother, William Rugg. He lives in Royal Exchange Lane, near King Street."

"I know of no such lane, and I am sure there is no such street as King Street in this town."

"Then," said he, "madam, can you direct me to Boston?"

"Why, this is the city of Boston. I know of no other Boston."

"City of Boston it may be, but it is not the Boston where I live. I recollect now, I came over a bridge instead of a ferry. Pray what bridge is that?"

"It is Charles River Bridge."

"I perceive my mistake; there is a ferry between Boston and Charlestown; there is no bridge. If I were in Boston my horse would carry me directly to my own door. But my horse shows by his impatience that he is in a strange place. Absurd, that I should have mistaken this place for the old town of Boston! It is a much finer city than the town of Boston."

At these words his horse began to chafe and strike the pavement with his fore-feet. The stranger seemed a little bewildered, and said, "No home to-night;" and giving the reins to his horse, passed up the street, and I saw no more of him.

This was all the account of Peter Rugg I could obtain from Mrs. Croft; but she directed me to an elderly man, James Felt, who lived near her, and who had kept a record of the principal occurrences for the last fifty years. Mr. Felt told me he had known Rugg in his youth; that his disappearance had caused some surprise; but as it sometimes happens that men run away, and Rugg had taken his child with him, and his own horse and chair, the occurrence was soon forgotten.

"Why, my friend," said James Felt, "that Peter Rugg is living I will not deny; but that you have seen him and his child is impossible, if you mean a small child, for Jenny Rugg, if living, must be at least — let me see, Boston Massacre, 1770 — Jenny Rugg was about ten years old. If living she must be more than sixty years of age. That Peter Rugg is living, is highly probable, as he was only ten years older than myself, and I was only eighty last March; and I am as likely to live twenty years longer as any man."

In the course of the evening I related my adventure in Middle Street. "Ha!" said one of the company, smiling, "do you really think you have seen Peter Rugg? I have heard my grandfather speak of him as though he seriously believed his own story. Peter Rugg once lived in Middle Street. His temper at times was altogether ungovernable; and then his language was terrible.

"It was late in autumn, one morning, that Rugg, in his own chair, with a fine large bay horse, took his daughter and proceeded to Concord. On his return a violent storm overtook him. At dark he stopped in Menotomy, now West Cambridge, at the door of a Mr. Cutter, a friend of his, who urged him to tarry the night. On Rugg's declining to stop, Cutter urged him vehemently. 'Why, Mr. Rugg,' said Cutter, 'the storm is overwhelming you; your little daughter will perish: you are in an open chair, and the tempest is increasing.' 'Let the storm increase,' said Rugg, with an oath; 'I will see home to-night, in spite of the last tempest, or may I never see home!' At these words he gave his whip to his high-spirited horse, and disappeared in a moment. But Peter Rugg did not reach home that night, or the next; nor, when he became a missing man, could he ever be traced beyond Cutter's in Menotomy.

There was a rumor that Rugg afterward was seen in Connecticut, between Suffield and Hartford, passing through the country with headlong speed. This gave occasion to Rugg's friends to make further inquiry. But the more they inquired, the more they were baffled. What added mystery to the story of Peter Rugg was the affair at Charlestown Bridge. The toll-gatherer asserted that sometimes on the darkest nights, when no object could be discerned, a horse and wheel carriage, with a noise equal to a troop, would at midnight, in utter contempt of the rates of toll, pass over the bridge. This occurred so frequently, that the toll-gatherer resolved to attempt a discovery. Soon after, at the usual time, apparently the same horse and carriage approached the bridge from Charlestown Square. The toll-gatherer took his stand near the middle of the bridge, with a large three-legged stool in his hand. As the apparition passed, he threw the stool at the horse, but heard nothing, except the noise of the stool skipping across the bridge. The next day he asserted that the stool went directly through the body of the horse; and he persisted in that belief ever after. Whether Rugg, or whoever the person was, ever passed the bridge again, the toll-gatherer would never tell; he seemed anxious to waive the subject. And thus Peter Rugg and his child, horse and carriage, remain a mystery to this day.

NANTUCKET LEGENDS

Nantucket is a great nursery of seamen, pilots, coasters, and bank-fishermen. The Friends compose two-thirds of the magistracy of this island; thus they are the proprietors of its territory and the principal rulers of its inhabitants; but with all this apparatus of law, its coercive powers are seldom wanted or required. Seldom is it that any individual is amerced or punished; their jail conveys no terror; no man has lost his life here judicially since the foundation of this town, which is upwards of a hundred years. The greatest part of them are always at sea, pursuing the whale or raising the cod from the surface of the banks.

J. HECTOR ST. JOHN DE CREVECOEUR, 1770

THE ISLANDS of Nantucket, Martha's Vineyard, and the Elizabeth group all possess more or less legendary lore that surrounds them with a peculiar fascination. One by one these islands have emerged from the sea into the light of history, and have taken a place upon the map. With caution their inhospitable coasts and foaming reefs were explored by the early navigators, and step by step Christian missionaries approached the fierce islanders who lived in happy ignorance that any other world than the neighboring mainland existed.

In the order of chronology it is the Elizabeth Islands that should be the first mentioned, since it was there that the bold attempt to found in New England a colony of Europeans was made. Vaguely conceived, not half matured, and feebly executed, it was abandoned in the very hour that should most fully test the mettle of those conducting it, and it is now memorable only because it was the first serious endeavor to naturalize Englishmen on the soil. Yet although these men left only a perishable footprint behind them, they did bestow enduring names on the capes and headlands that rose out of the sea to greet them. So far as known, however, not one is a memento of themselves; nevertheless it is these names that have rendered the voyage of Bartholomew Gosnold a feat worth preserving. In the whole company of thirty-two that set sail with him from Falmouth only twelve intended to remain in the country as settlers.

From Falmouth, on March 25, 1602, the *Concord* put to sea. On Friday, May 14, Gosnold had in view the lumpy coast of New England, stretching from Agamenticus to Cape Ann; and presently, to the great wonder of all on board — for these English could not believe that any had preceded them here — they fell in with a Basque shallop, manned by eight tawny, black-haired natives, who could speak a few English words intelligibly, and could name Placentia, in Newfoundland. It seemed that these savages had communicated with the French there. Gosnold now put his helm to starboard, and steering southward into the Bay found himself brought to by the bended forearm of the great sandspit to which he gave the name of Cape Cod. He continued cautiously working his way along the south coast, shortening sail at night, until he was again embayed within the chain of islands extending

The shoreline at Gay Head, of Martha's Vineyard, named by Gosnold
for an unidentified woman

Elihu Coleman raised this house in 1772 on Nantucket

between Buzzard's Bay and the open sea — a broken, but still magnificent barrier. One of these he called Martha's Vineyard, thinking so little of the matter that he left nothing to satisfy the curiosity of another age respecting the person he had meant to honor. Thus Martha's Vineyard remains a monument with an incomplete inscription which nobody is able to clarify.

Eleven days after sighting the coast the adventurers landed on Cuttyhunk Island, to which Gosnold gave the name of Elizabeth, the Queen, a name since applied to the whole group. They decided to make this island their residence.

Having great fear of the savages, Gosnold's men set to work building a fort, in which they dwelt until they had procured a cargo of sassafras, when they hurriedly decamped and set sail for England. On the grand scheme of colonization of which this was to be the entering wedge, this voyage had no further result than to act as a spur to the lords proprietors, who impoverished themselves in fruitless efforts, until the year 1620 showed them what might be done without other resources than courage, persistency, and a firm reliance on the assistance of heaven.

Gosnold also saw and named the remarkable promontory of Gay Head, probably so called from its brilliant and variegated coloring when the sun shone full upon it. The structure of this lofty headland bears evidences of its volcanic origin. Four or five craters are more or less distinctly traced. The most ancient of these, called the Devil's Den, measures twenty rods across at the top, fourteen at the bottom, and is one hundred and thirty feet deep at the sides, except upon the one next the sea, which is open. The most fantastic stories were told about this spot until the beginning of the 19th century; for here was one of the residences of Maushope, the Indian giant, the tutelary genius of all the tribes inhabiting these islands and the adjacent mainland of Cape Cod. Like Fingal, Maushope was in the habit of wading across the Sound when the humor took him. Here he broiled the whale on coals made from the largest trees, which he pulled up by the roots. After separating No-man's Land from Gay Head, metamorphosing his children into fishes, and throwing his wife on Seconnet Point, where she now lies, a misshapen rock, he broke up housekeeping and left for parts unknown.

The fishermen used to say that it was a common thing to see a light on Gay Head in the night-time, and it was handed down that the whalemen were in the habit of guiding themselves at night by the lights that were seen glancing on Gay Head. When they appeared flickering in the darkness the sailors would say, "Old Maushope is at it again!" But the beacon-lights were held to be friendly ones; for, like the stars, they showed the belated mariner what course to steer. The sea has encroached greatly upon the clay cliffs in the course of centuries. The harmless descendants of the warlike race still inhabit the place; but the light shining from a massive tower has superseded the midnight orgies of the wandering Maushope.

Like the Eastern wizards, Maushope was capable of raising mists whenever he wished; but that his was wholly an original method will appear from the following traditional account of the discovery of Nantucket, which is presented *verbatim.*

"In former times, a great many moons ago, a bird, extraordinary for its size, used often to visit the south shore of Cape Cod and carry from thence in its talons a vast number of small children. Maushope, who was an Indian giant, as fame reports, resided in these parts. Enraged at the havoc among the children, he on a certain time waded into the sea in pursuit of the bird, till he had crossed the Sound and reached Nantucket. Before Maushope forded the Sound the island was unknown to the red men. Maushope found the bones of the children in a heap under a large tree. He then, wishing to smoke a pipe, ransacked the island for tobacco; but finding none, he filled his pipe with poke, — a weed which the Indians sometimes used as a substitute. Ever since the above memorable events fogs have been frequent at Nantucket and on the Cape. In allusion to this tradition, when the aborigines observed a fog rising, they would say, 'There comes old Maushope's smoke!' This tradition has been related in another way: that an eagle having seized and carried off a papoose, the parents followed him in their canoe till they came to Nantucket, where they found the bones of their child dropped by the eagle. There is another Indian tradition, that Nantucket was formed by Maushope by emptying the ashes from his pipe after he had done smoking. The two tribes on the island were hostile to each other. Tradition has preserved a pleasing instance of the power of love. The western tribe having determined to surprise and attack the eastern tribe, a young man of the former, whose mistress belonged to the latter, being anxious for her safety, as soon as he was concealed by the shades of night, ran to the beach, flew along the shore below the limit of high water, saw his mistress a moment, gave the alarm, and returned by the same route before daybreak; the rising tide washed away the traces of his feet. Th next morning he accompanied the other warriors of the tribe to the attack: the enemy was found prepared, and no impression could be made on them. He remained undetected till, several years after, peace being restored between the two tribes, and the young man having married the girl, the truth came to light."

We have elsewhere related the circumstances that led to the settlement of Nantucket by the whites. The Quaker element long

The Rotch Market and Drinking Fountain, Nantucket. *Right*, South Tower in Old Nantucket

continued to be dominant in the social life of the island, as well as in its religion and government. Here, free from persecution, these much-abused followers of George Fox were supposed to have found their Arcadia. They established a patriarchal government. Instead of laws, they had usages which were obeyed as laws. It was nearly the happy ideal condition, where men live without quarrels, without crime, and without the enforcement of law. They were husbandmen and shepherds. They fished, planted, and traded in peace. Although some of them amassed wealth, everything about them continued to wear the appearance of a primitive economy; they lived on independently and prosperously. But notwithstanding a natural predilection for the land — and we can hardly think of Quakers as making good sailors — there was the sea continually asserting itself at their doors. By a transition as curious as it is absolute, these peaceful shepherds became most noted sailors and the

Two Starbock Houses at Nantucket

most renowned whalemen of the world. With this change the native Indians doubtless had much to do; for in their primitive way they too were expert in taking whales. The Nantucket whale-fishery began in the waters immediately surrounding the island, and in boats. The whaleman finished his career amid the Arctic ice, where he quietly made for himself a route long before governments entered into the disastrous contest with King Frost in which so many valuable lives have been lost. Had there been certain indications that whales were to be found at the Pole, the Nantucket whalemen would have discovered it.

The sea annals of Nantucket are consequently numerous, and as they relate chiefly to stubborn conflicts with whales, they are very interesting. But as we now get our oil on the land, the industry that brought Nantucket into world-wide notice no longer has any existence there. There is, however, a museum, in which are preserved many evidences to the fact, in the same manner that Salem preserves the memorials of her departed East Indian trade. The whale-fishery gave to the nation a race of intrepid sailors, who might have become at need her defenders: the petroleum discovery has given us some millionnaires.

Thomas Macy, the Exile of Nantucket

Thomas Macy, yeoman of Salisbury, in the county of Essex, who has been described as the first settler of Nantucket, undeservedly became a hero when John Greenleaf Whittier, exercising his customary freedom with a theme, embellished his behavior in a poem. The hero of the poem was accused of having given shelter to some notorious Quakers, or vagabonds, as the law termed them, in his own house. For this act of hospitality in violation of the law prohibiting any man to open his door to a Quaker, Macy was cited to appear forthwith before the General Court at Boston. According to the legend Wharton and two other Quakers were sheltered by Macy when a troop of horsemen arrived determined to take them, "Bold Macy" defied the burly sheriff, and when the latter attempted to seize him also, fled with his wife to the shore, entered a boat and sailed to Nantucket, by way of Cape Ann and Cape Cod. Before leaving Macy taunted the sheriff with such insults as: "Whip women on the village green but meddle not with men!" When the Macys reach Nantucket, "a refuge of the free," the poet apostrophizes the place: "God bless the sea-beat island, and grant for evermore that charity and freedom dwell as now upon her shore."

But the brave stand of Macy does not tally with the actual record. Instead of complying with the requisition, which few would be found willing to disobey, Macy wrote a humble, apologetic and deprecatory letter to the General Court. The letter indicates a man of very different stamp from the antique hero that Whittier's poem depicts in the act of cheating the law of its prey. Its terms do not show that Bold Macy was cast in the mold of martyrs and that, if not actually a craven, he preferred discretion. The letter to the General Court reads:

This is to entreat the honored court not to be offended because of my non-appearance. It is not from any slighting the authority of this honored court, nor from feare to answer the case, but I have bin for some weeks past very ill, and am so at present, and notwithstanding my illness, yet I, desirous to appear, have done my utmost endeavour to hire a horse, but cannot procure one at present. I being at present destitute have endeavoured to purchase, but at present cannot attaine it, but I shall relate the truth of the case as my answer should be to ye honored court, and more cannot be proved, nor so much. On a rainy morning there came to my house Edward Wharton and three men more; the said Wharton spoke to me, saying that they were traveling eastward, and desired me to direct them in the way to Hampton, and asked me how far it was to Casco bay. I never saw any of ye men afore except Wharton, neither did I require their names, or who they were, but by their carriage I thought they might be Quakers, and told them so, and therefore desired them to passe on their way, saying to them I might possibly give offence in entertaining them, and as soone as the violence of the rain ceased (for it rained very hard) they went away, and I never saw them since. The time that they stayed in the house was about three quarters of an hour, but I can safely affirme it was not an hour. They spake not many words in the time, neither was I at leisure to talke with them, for I came home wet to the skin immediately afore they came to the house, and I found my wif sick in bed. If this satisfie not the honored court, I shall subject to their sentence. I have not willingly offended. I am ready to serve and obey you in the Lord.   THO. MACY

Three of these men, being preachers, could look for no mercy from the Puritan authorities, who charged them with going about seducing his Majesty's subjects to their "cursed" opinions. One of them, Edward Wharton, was an old offender. Two of them, Robinson and Stevenson, are the same persons who, a little later on, were hanged at Boston. These itinerants undoubtedly knew where to apply, and to whom. Macy knew Wharton; he was fully aware of the risk he ran in breaking the law. But he and other Quakers of Newbury and Salisbury already had purchased the island of Nantucket, to which they probably intended removing out of harm's way, as that island was not within the jurisdiction of the Massachusetts Bay Colony.

Thus Macy had secured an asylum in advance, and when the General Court refused to allow his explanation or accept his apology, Macy and his wife took an open boat, put their children and their movable effects into it, and in this frail conveyance made their way to Nantucket. Edward Starbock, of Salisbury, accompanied them. Through persecution, then, Macy became the first white inhabitant of this island, and from his landing at Maddequet in the autumn of 1659 the settlement dates its history.

TRAGEDY AT BLOCK ISLAND

B LOCK ISLAND is a bank of clay, treeless and wind-swept, eight
miles long, rising out of the ocean between Montauk and
Gay Head, and lying nearest to Point Judith, on the Rhode Island
shore, five miles distant. Planted athwart the highway of a vast
commerce, it was a dangerous obstacle in the days of sail. In clear
weather its brilliant light cheered the grateful mariner on his
voyage with its signal of "All's well, and a fine night!"

A tribe of the warlike Narragansetts once inhabited this sea-
girt isle, to which their fathers gave the euphonious name of
Manisses. But powerful as they were, they were also a race of plun-
derers, traits common to islanders, so that their thieving propensi-
ties brought down upon them the vengeance of the whites, who
made an armed descent upon the island with the purpose of ex-
terminating every warrior on it. Before the wars were over, the
island passed forever from the Indians, who had fled from it in
terror, taking a civilized name from the Dutch sailor Adrian Block,
and subsequently that of New Shoreham, which the township still
retains.

Then began the gradual settlement of the island and a development, sometimes checked by the wars. Because it was available for pasturage, the islanders were mostly farmers, who raised cattle, sheep, and poultry for the mainland. This was gradually superseded by tillage.

Those who were not farmers were fishermen. The seas around the island teemed with cod, mackerel, and blue fish, thus furnishing subsistence to another class, who toiled with net and line, and who built their rude cabins and flakes by the shore. But as the island lacked a good harbor, fishing and trading went on by boats in the old primitive way.

The reputation of the island was never good. It had a bad lee shore, a place of no good hap for the unlucky mariner who might be driven upon it, and there were dark hints, and still darker traditions, concerning shipwrecked crews and valuable cargoes. "I would rather be wrecked anywhere than upon Block Island," became a common and significant saying in the forecastle when the dark mass of the island heaved in sight. But all this refers to long ago; for though there were still wreckers in the nineteenth century their work proceeded with some regard for the saving of life and the lawful claims of owners. In "the good old times" the wreckers stripped a ship and divided her cargo on the principle that to the finders belongs the spoil. "Everything is fish," said they, "that comes to our net."

Like all islanders, these people were generally hardy, sober, and industrious. But a difference was to be observed between the farmers and the fishermen, — a name often synonymous with that of wreckers or smugglers. So isolated were they from the rest of the world that intermarriage of those more or less related by blood was a thing of common occurrence. The result was thought unfavorable to the physical condition of the islanders and an instance was mentioned of a woman who left three deaf-and-dumb sons at her death.

Some time during the eighteenth century, the *Palatine*, an emigrant ship bound for Philadelphia, reached the American coast, only to be driven off to sea again by stress of weather. The emigrants were thrifty Dutch people who had brought all their property with them to their new home, whither many of their countrymen had preceded them. Some of them are said to have been wealthy. It was in the dark and dreary season of midwinter. With the coast in sight but unable to gain her port, the ship, buffeting the frozen seas, was driven northward far out of her course. The captain had died, or had been murdered at sea, before the vessel came in sight of the land. All discipline was at an end, and the ship's crew began a system of cold-blooded robbery. The wretches armed themselves; and having taken possession of the water and provisions, with a refined cruelty demanded from the famishing emigrants twenty Dutch guilders for a cup of water, and fifty rix-dollars for a biscuit. To save their lives the passengers were obliged to beggar themselves. Those who could not or would not comply with the atrocious demand were condemned to starve, and their emaciated bodies were thrown into the sea. The ship soon became a floating hell. Having plundered their victims of everything of value, the inhuman crew finally took to the boats and left the ship to the mercy of winds and waves. With no one left on board to navigate her, the doomed ship drifted on. Days of despair were succeeded by nights of horror. She was now a madhouse, tenanted only by maniacs or the unburied corpses of those who had died from famine or disease.

One calm Sabbath morning the *Palatine* struck on the northernmost reef of Block Island. But her voyage was not to end here. The wreckers of the island manned their boats and rescued all those who had survived starvation, except one woman, who had gone stark mad and refused to leave the wreck.

The ship, having only touched the reef, floated off again with the rising tide, and the wreckers made their boats fast, and towed her into a neighboring cove, to dismantle her at their leisure. Before this could be done a gale sprang up; and the wreckers, seeing that the ship would be blown off to sea, set her on fire.

New England Coast

Enveloped in flames from truck to deck, the *Palatine* drove out into the darkness of a stormy sea, an object of dread even to those who had so recklessly applied the torch. But this feeling was turned to deeper horror when frenzied shrieks from the burning ship told those on shore that a human being was perishing miserably in the flames. These sounds were supposed to proceed from the madwoman, who had been forgotten. The *Palatine* drifted away and burned to the water's edge.

Years afterward the islanders asserted that on the anniversary of the storm, they were affrighted by the spectacle of a ship on fire in the offing, which, as the gale rose, drifted before it and gradually faded from their sight, exactly as the *Palatine* had done. Year after year the same strange sight continued to keep the fate of the ship fresh in the memory of the islanders, who became convinced that this annual visitation was a portent of disaster to them. The tradition became established, and although skeptics related the apparition to the inevitable mists, the legend was repeated as fact and eventually enshrined in poetry.

ANCIENT RELICS
IN NEW ENGLAND

More than one hundred years ago Samuel Adams Drake was adding to his collection of legends speculation about reputed evidence of pre-Columbian remains in New England. So were dozens of other writers, and down to this day archaeologists differ sharply about the origin of the Old Stone Tower at Newport, Rhode Island, which Philip Ainsworth Means concluded was a Norse church. In 1965 new evidence of Norse voyages across the Atlantic became public when Yale University Press issued Vinland: The Tartar Relation, *by R. A. Skelton, based on a map antedating Columbus. In the following account Drake describes the 19th-century consensus about Newport Tower, Dighton Rock, and other evidence. It is worth noting that while Drake expressed skepticism about the conclusions of Danish archaeologists of his time, it was a Danish investigator whose reports to Smithsonian Institution in 1950 agreed with Drake. The origin of the Newport Tower, however, remains uncertain. That Governor Arnold in his will called it "my stone mill" is accepted, but the remains of a fireplace on the second tier continue to baffle investigators.*

LONGFELLOW's ballad of *The Skeleton in Armor* is the legitimate product of one of those obscure traditions which, through frequent repetition, acquire all the consistency of authentic facts; yet, like other illusions, disappear as soon as the light is turned on them. In this case the Scandinavian tradition recounts the adventurous voyages of the two Norse corsairs, Leif and Thorwald, to the new world as early as A.D. 1000. They are said to have sailed from Iceland, and to have passed a winter in the western hemisphere.

The terms of these sagas are so ambiguous, even should they be accounted true relations, as to render extremely difficult attempts to trace the voyages they narrate, with the purpose of fitting them to our own coasts or harbors. The Danish antiquarians would be deeply interested in establishing the validity of the claim on the part of their countrymen to a discovery preceding Columbus by nearly five centuries was only natural, for should they succeed it would prove the most brilliant feat in their maritime history. The relations themselves, however, are vague, and without stronger evidence the reputable historian would certainly hesitate long, and examine critically, before installing the vague and the veritable side by side. Should he positively declare America to have been discovered by the Northmen in the year 1000, he must first withdraw the assertion made in favor of the illustrious Genoese to a discovery in 1492.

Several things contributed to produce in the public mind an effect favorable to the Scandinavian claim. The most important of these were the alleged evidences then existing of an occupation of the country by the Norse voyagers. There was, and still is, at Newport in Rhode Island, an old windmill of peculiar, and for New England unique, construction, which time has left a picturesque ruin. The main structure of stone presents the appearance of a round tower thirty feet high, supported by massive stone columns, also round; for the woodwork having fallen away, nothing but the bare walls remain to identify its original form or purpose. It stands

on the heights overlooking the harbor, and until time's changes hid
it from view, was always a conspicuous object when the city was
approached from the sea. This structure had been so long unused
that little importance need be attached to the fact that the purpose
for which it was originally built had gradually died out of the
memory of the oldest inhabitant. Its proper functions having so
long ceased, no one regarded it except with a feeble curiosity, nor
was there even a local tradition concerning it. For a century and a
half it had stood on the same spot without a question arising as to
its origin; it was completely ignored. But at length some one discovered a resemblance to Scandinavian architecture. The Danish
savans at once claimed the windmill as the work of their countrymen centuries before the arrival of the English.

There was also on the shore of Taunton River, a tidal stream
that flows into Narragansett Bay, and might therefore be easily
ascended by an exploring vessel, a moderately large bowlder,
one face of which, being smooth, was completely covered with mysterious hieroglyphics which no one had been able to decipher. The
strange characters originally had been deeply cut into the perpen-
dicular face toward the channel; but in the course of years, and
owing to the rock itself being partly submerged at high tide, the
continual abrasion of water and ice has nearly obliterated them;
so that it is now scarcely possible to identify these marks as the
work of human hands. The bowlder received the name of Dighton
Rock because the shore where it lay imbedded was within the limits of the town of Dighton. Here was a veritable relic of antiquity.
Unlike the Newport tower, this had always been the subject of
eager curiosity and discussion, so much so, that copies of the
inscription had been transmitted by Cotton Mather to the learned
societies of London as a valuable contribution to the purposes of
archaeological research; while the Newport structure, notwithstanding its alleged peculiarity of construction and possible proof
of the residence here of Europeans so long ago, was not thought
to be worthy of such study. The sculptured rock remained, how-

The Old Stone Tower in Newport, Rhode Island

ever, an unsolved enigma. A vague local tradition only rendered it all the more perplexing. It is true that many who were acquainted with the rude commemorative drawings by Indians, which those of the rock greatly resembled, believed the Indians had at some time cut the characters. This natural solution of the mystery became the subject of controversy. The Danish antiquarians, better instructed, declared Dighton Rock to be a record of the adventurous voyages of their countrymen.

Still another event obtained for the theory a certain amount of sympathy, thus giving it a strength of a wholly different kind in the popular mind. Hitherto the new idea had taken less with the general public than with scholars; the materials were now found for a veritable *coup de théâtre*.

There was exhumed at Fall River the skeleton of a man whose chest was protected by an oval plate of brass, and on whose fleshless thighs still loosely hung a belt of curious workmanship, made of hollow tubes of brass much corroded, and fitted together in the manner of the bandoliers worn when firearms were in their infancy. There were also found near the skeleton some arrow-heads made of the same metal. It is true that the body had been buried in a sitting posture, with its arms and ornaments, agreeable to the funeral customs of the Indians of this coast. It is also true that from the voyages of the Cabots down to the coming in of the English settlers here, the possession of copper ornaments, and even weapons of war, by the Indians, was a fact constantly repeated. Even the chains and collars, one of which was worn by the skeleton, had been exactly and minutely described in some of the *Relations* by Hakluyt. But the sagas had said that Thorwald, the Norse rover-chief, was slain in an encounter with the natives, and had been hastily interred near the spot where he fell. The breast-plate and arrows were said to be identical with those in use among the Scandinavians of this ancient period. To the silent evidence of the tower and the rock was now joined that of a supposed Norse warrior in his armor.

The case as it now stood may be briefly summed up. A building said to be of a construction similar to the most ancient ones in the Scandinavian peninsula, not dating later than the twelfth century, certainly unlike anything of British architecture, had been found; a rock inscribed with possibly Runic characters had been discovered; a skeleton wearing armor of the kind used by Norse warriors had been disinterred, and these things existed within such neighborhood to each other as to constitute a chain of evidence strong in itself, strengthened by probability, and further supported by the general feeling in its favor, that they were the work or the remains of the Norsemen. To such an array, presented with such authority and with so much confidence, it is no wonder that the sceptical at first were confused.

But each of these pieces of evidence has been fully disproved. It has been shown that the Newport Tower was of a build similar to that of a stone mill in Chesterton, England. The attempt to convert the characters of Dighton Rock into Runic, or even into an intelligible historic record of any kind, signally failed to convince either learned or unlearned. And lastly, the metal found upon the skeleton turned out to be different from that used for warlike purposes by the ancient Scandinavians. To this the direct evidence that a windmill stood on the spot where the ruin now stands; that Governor Arnold mentions it in his will; that the way leading to it is still called Mill Street; and that it was commonly known as a windmill and nothing else, would seem finally to dispose of what was left of the Northmen's antique tower, and to leave it the simple and striking memorial of the forefathers.

In a note to *The Skeleton in Armor* Longfellow says that he considers the tradition sufficiently established for the purpose of a ballad. But he naïvely adds what few will now be found willing to dispute, that, "doubtless many an honest citizen of Newport, who has passed his days within sight of the round tower, will be ready to exclaim, with Sancho: 'God bless me! did I not warn you to have a care what you were doing, for that it was nothing but a windmill; and nobody could mistake it but one who had the like in his head.'" But the subject remains open to debate, and no final decision has ever been reached.

An oblique vista of the Pioneer Village, Salem

INDEX

Titles of illustrations and names of ships in italics

190   INDEX